WOODWORKER TO

LIVE EDGE SLABS

Transforming Trees into Tables, Benches, Cutting Boards, and More

WOODWORKER'S GUIDE TO LIVE EDGE SLABS

Transforming Trees into Tables, Benches, Cutting Boards, and More

GEORGE VONDRISKA

Fox Chapel
PUBLISHING
www.FoxChapelPublishing.com

ISBN 978-1-4971-0143-2

Library of Congress Control Number: 2021939763

To learn more about the other great books from Fox Chapel Publishing, or to find a retailer near you, call toll-free 800-457-9112 or visit us at *www.FoxChapelPublishing.com*.

We are always looking for talented authors. To submit an idea, please send a brief inquiry to acquisitions@foxchapelpublishing.com.

Printed in Singapore
First printing

Introduction

Many woodworking projects call for material that's been highly processed: typically planks of wood cut to a specific thickness and width. The project dictates the material used, and how it should be used. Working with live edge slabs is different. Instead of the project dictating the material, a slab tells me what project it should best be used for. I love this. A live edge slab is still, in large part, the tree it came from. The edges are irregular, bark may still be attached, it may have knots, bug holes or splits. On conventional woodworking projects I generally cut around those "defects." On live edge slab projects, I embrace and highlight them. The projects I create with slabs look and feel like they're still a part of the tree. This makes working with slabs so much fun! Every live edge slab I touch is a little different from the last, and the discovery process is part of the fun.

This book provides you with the woodworking techniques you need to start working with live edge slabs, along with a number of projects you can use as a jumping off point. I want this book to give you the excitement I feel each time I see a slab, along with the wonder of "What does that slab want to become?"

Table of Contents

72

98

106

116

42

132

124

90

Author's Gallery

Endless Inspiration

The natural beauty of wood really comes through when you're working with slabs. These are a few of my favorite slab-based pieces. When you marry the right piece of wood with the right form, you get a useful, wonderfully unique piece of furniture.

Soft maple desk with painted poplar base
29" tall x 24" x 42"

Pine side table with walnut
butterfly 32" tall x 18" x 72"

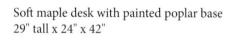

Pine coffee table with
walnut bowties 16" tall
32" diameter

Burr oak side table
18" tall 24" diameter

Pine coffee table
16" tall x 20" x 48"

Pine coffee table
16" tall x 18" x 48"

Douglas fir side table
30" tall x 18" x 24"

Walnut coffee table with spalted
maple bowtie 16" tall x 23" x 48"

Figured hard maple desk
29" tall x 28" x 52"

Cherry side table with walnut
bowties 16" tall x 14" x 32"

Figured hard maple coffee table
16" tall x 20" x 48"

Soft maple kitchen table and benches
Table 30" tall x 36" x 60"
Benches 16" tall x 14" x 60"

Bookmatched hard maple burl side table
28" tall x 20" x 30"

Maker's Gallery

Austin Heitzman

A man of many influences, from a love of nature to growing up in Southeast Asia to a day job at the Philadelphia Museum of Art, Austin Heitzman's furniture is a true celebration of materials.

His creations flow from the locally-salvaged city trees he seeks out in his home of Portland, OR, including unique species such as apple, plum, and English walnut. In his words, "Nature does most of the work; I simply let it guide my hand."

You can learn more about Heitzman on his website at austinheitzmanfurniture.com.

PHOTOS COURTESY OF THE ARTIST.

Above:

Heitzman's dished coffee table marries an inset, circular piece of glass on a slice of live edge walnut burl.

Right:

This liquor cabinet puts both the beautiful slab and a decanter front and center. Inside, there's illuminated glass shelving that doesn't hide the beauty of the wood (or the liquor).

Thomas Throop

Based in New Canaan, CT, Throop has been designing and making custom furniture since 1992. He aims to create work that both serves his clients' functional needs while also showcasing beautiful materials and unique forms. He grew up building boats and repairing antiques with his uncle in the summer. After college, Throop spent several years restoring old homes before heading to England to study with John Makepeace.

While his work is deeply rooted in the expression of wood and old world craftsmanship, the work is still ultimately contemporary. You can learn more about his work at blackcreekdesigns.com.

PHOTOS COURTESY OF THE ARTIST.

Throop's Pine Point bed uses a slab as the focal point.

The Kagan table features geometric inlay and coopered legs.

Supported by gently curving legs, the Beck desk has a small drawer to make it a truly functional work of art.

Jess Crow

This Alaska-based maker uses natural edge wood as the base for her handmade pieces of art. Crow has pioneered a unique epoxy painting techniques that gives her furniture and objects a truly handcrafted, one-of-a-kind look.

Her proudly woman-owned and run woodworking shop is a leading authority in artistic woodworking and epoxy. She even developed her own formula of epoxy called MakerPoxy, for her intricate, creative painted slab work.

You can learn more about Crow and working with epoxy at crowcreekdesigns.com.

PHOTOS COURTESY OF THE ARTIST.

Above:

Crow's Salmon bed includes a slab headboard with an epoxy-painted scene flowing through the center.

Right:

The live-edge Stream coffee table puts a rendering of fish in motion center stage. Both water and fish are recurring themes in Crow's work.

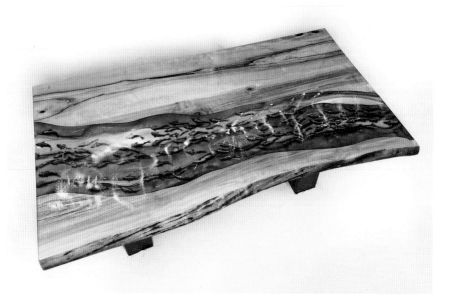

Cremona's take on the classic twin bed makes ample use of live edges, including along the bed rail.

Below:

Three waterfall coffee tables. On the left, the void is stabilized and filled with epoxy. On the right, the void is covered with a custom fit piece of glass.

Matt Cremona

Today, all of Matt Cremona's work starts at the custom, extra-wide sawmill he built in his suburban Minnesota yard, where he processes urban lumber into slabs. Though not all of his work is truly live-edge in the literal sense, he starts at the slab, using all the different kinds of grain running through a slab to match the parts of his furniture – very rarely does a milled, four-square board make it into his shop.

A self-taught woodworker, he quit his computer job to focus on milling lumber, woodworking, and creating videos to inspire others to make things.

You can learn more about Cremona and get plans to build your own extra-wide sawmill at mattcremona.com.

PHOTOS COURTESY OF THE ARTIST.

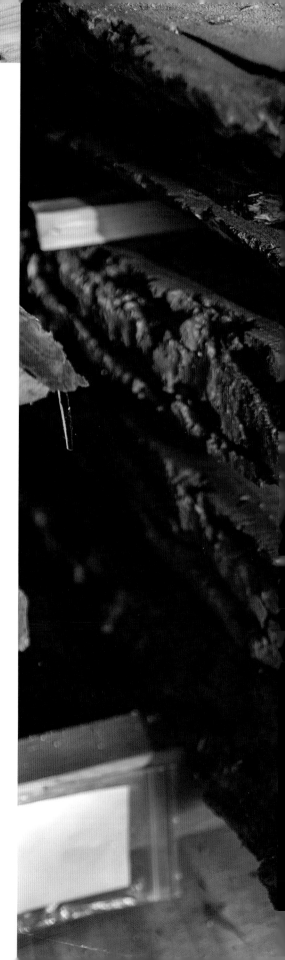

Logs to Lumber

As a woodworker, it's important to understand
how logs get processed into lumber and how the
resulting material is dried. This information will
not only make you a more educated consumer,
but it will also help you ensure that you get what
you pay for when you buy lumber and help you
determine if lumber you buy is ready to be used.

Understanding the milling and drying process
will also help if you mill your own lumber using
a bandsaw or chainsaw and help ensure that your
labor results in good material. Even if you can
easily purchase lumber, cutting your own is fun
and allows you to mill species of wood you may
not be able to get commercially.

Cutting and Drying

1. With the log positioned on the bandsaw mill, slabs are cut from the top face. The log remains stationary, and the bandsaw is propelled through it. The mill can be set to produce any desired thickness of material.

2. Air drying wood is simple, but requires patience. A general rule of thumb is to allow it to dry for one year per inch of thickness. It should be stacked in a place where air can easily flow over it, and it's best if it isn't in direct sun.

Sawmills commonly use a circular saw or bandsaw to process logs. Both methods work equally well. Bandsaw mills, **Photo 1**, are a little more common. Logs are cut while they're still wet, which is commonly referred to as green. This is important. If a log is allowed to dry it will probably split to a point that it's unusable. Plus, dry wood is harder to cut than wet wood. Referring to wood as wet or green means the wood contains a lot of water. Wet wood isn't suitable for projects because, as it dries, the wood will crack, shrink and distort. The amount of water in wood is expressed as a percentage, called moisture content. If the moisture content is 30%, 30% of the log's weight is water, 70% is wood.

The moisture content of freshly cut logs can exceed 20%. As a general rule of thumb, wood needs to dry to 8% to 14% moisture content before it can be used for indoor furniture. A simple, low tech, approach is to air dry the wood, **Photo 2**. The wood is stacked with spacers, called stickers, between each layer so air can flow through the pile and over the wood. The end grain is often sealed with paint or a drying-specific sealer. Air drying generally brings wood to 12% – 14% moisture content, which is fine for live edge furniture.

Wood can also be kiln dried. It's stickered and placed in a large oven, **Photo 3**. Kiln drying brings the moisture content down to about 6% – 8% All wood, no matter how it's dried, will expand and contract seasonally. It's important to take wood movement into account in your projects. It's also important to allow wood to acclimate to your environment. Do this by bringing material into your shop at least a few days before starting your projects.

3. On a commercial scale wood is often kiln dried. This is much faster than air drying, often complete in a few weeks.

If you buy slabs directly from a sawmill you can get sequence cut slabs, meaning they were next to each other in the log. This results in bookmatched pieces, meaning that the wood grain is mirrored from one piece to the next.

Common Cuts

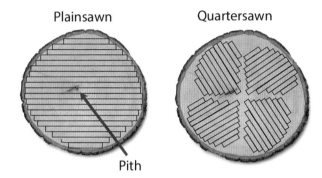

4. The two most common methods of cutting lumber are plainsawn and quartersawn. Quartersawn is more labor intensive to cut, and has more waste, so it's usually more expensive to purchase than plainsawn.

The two most common approaches for milling lumber are plainsawn and quartersawn, **Photo 4**. Plainsawn lumber is the most common by a long shot. Depending on where the board comes from in the log, it can be more prone to cupping and warping than quartersawn lumber, but plainsawn lumber is much easier to cut and produces less waste. In addition to being more dimensionally stable, quartersawn wood, in some species, can produce a more attractive grain pattern.

Making Your Own Lumber

On a smaller scale, you can mill your own lumber using a bandsaw or chainsaw. The resulting live edge boards can become shelves, charcuterie boards, or other small projects.

For best results, be sure the log you're milling is still green. Try to mill the log as soon as possible after the tree is cut down. If the bark is still on, leave it on. That will prevent the log from drying too fast and cracking. Paint the end grain of the log with latex paint or end grain sealer. This will help slow down the drying rate if you're not able to cut the log right away, and it needs to be done to seal the ends of the sawn boards anyway for drying. It's much easier to seal the end of the log than a bunch of the ends of individual boards.

Bandsaw Milled Lumber

The size of log you can mill with your bandsaw will depend on how heavy a log you can pick up, and on the capacity of your bandsaw. Many woodworkers find they can cut logs up to about 12" in diameter and 30" long, depending on the capacity of their bandsaws. It's helpful to have another pair of hands available for larger logs. They're heavy.

The first step in bandsaw milling a log is to create flat reference surfaces on opposing faces of the log using a hand-held planer or belt sander, **Photo 5**.

5. Flat spots on the bottom and top of the log prevent it from rolling as you cut it, and give you a place to easily put a line you can follow when cutting.

Don't try to cut a log without a flat spot on the bottom. It could roll during the cut, which is very dangerous. If the bark is smooth you could skip the flat spot on top of the log. Using a chalk line, snap a

6. Snap a line on top of the log. This line should be in line with the pith on both ends of the log.

7. Freehand cut the log, following the chalk line. Use a 2-4 TPI (teeth per inch) blade, as wide as your saw will handle.

8. After the first cut, use the fence on your bandsaw to guide the material as you cut planks from the log.

line on top of the log, **Photo 6**. Align the chalk line with the pith (the bullseye) at the center of the log's growth rings. This won't necessarily be the center of the log. Cut the log on your bandsaw, **Photo 7**, following the chalk line.

You may find it helpful to have someone on hand to help catch the log halves as they exit the bandsaw.

With that first cut done, set your bandsaw fence to your desired lumber thickness and cut the planks, **Photo 8**. The wood will shrink as it dries, and you'll surface it to clean it up, so cut the boards at least ¼" thicker than the finished thickness you want.

Chainsaw Milled Lumber

A chainsaw provides a really fast way to turn logs into lumber. If you're planning on milling lots of lumber with a chainsaw, it's worth investing in a ripping chain. Ripping chains have different tooth geometry than crosscut chains and are easier to use for rip cuts. But if you're only doing this once in a while, a sharp standard crosscut chain works just fine.

Lay the log on its side on a pair of 4x4s and mark out your cuts on one end of the log, **Photo 9**. The 4x4s prevent the log from rolling. As you mark out the thickness of the boards take into account the fact that the chainsaw's kerf (the material removed as you cut) is quite wide at about ⅜".

Cut on the lines that you created, **Photo 10**. Don't cut all the way through the log. Stop 1" above the bottom. Cutting a log with the bar parallel to the grain, as shown, is much easier than cutting from the end grain down. If the log is longer than your bar, you can cut from both ends, **Photo 11**.

Finish the cuts by standing the log on end on top of the 4x4s and cutting vertically through the 1" of wood you left on the ripping cuts, **Photo 12**. It's hard to get great cut quality from a handheld chainsaw, so it's a good idea to mill the boards extra thick so there's plenty of room to clean them up.

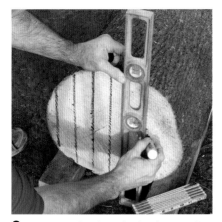

9. Position a level so it's plumb, straight up and down, and use a felt tip marker to create cut lines on the end of the log. The level guarantees that the lines are parallel to each other.

10. Cut the log, following your lines as best you can.

11. Cut from both ends when the log is longer than your bar. When cutting from the second, unmarked, end follow the kerfs created by cuts you did from the marked end.

Drying

Seal the ends of the boards with latex paint or end grain sealer, **Photo 13**. Stack the boards to allow them to air dry, **Photo 14**. This can take quite a while. Put them in a place where air can move over the stack. Plywood scraps work well for stickers. The best way to monitor the drying is by using a moisture meter. If, after a few days of measurements, the moisture content is consistent (generally 12% to 14%) the planks have reached equilibrium and are dry. A general rule of thumb is that it will take one year per inch of thickness for the green wood to dry, 2" boards will take two years to dry. This varies depending on where you live and the environment you're drying them in. That also underscores the importance of using a moisture meter. The moisture meter provides an accurate way to measure moisture content so you're not guessing.

12. Stand the log on end on the 4x4s and cut through the 1" of material remaining from the rip cuts.

13. The end grain on each board needs to be sealed with latex paint or end grain sealer.

14. Stack and sticker the boards and give them ample time to dry.

Prep Your Slabs

Slabs for your projects will, in all likelihood, need some work to be made ready to use. They might still be wet, rough sawn, not perfectly flat, or (likely) all of the above. You'll need to do some work on the slab in your shop.

Moisture Content

1. It's imperative to check the moisture content of slabs before you use them.

Flattening Your Slabs

2. Check your slab with a straightedge to see if it's flat. If not, you'll need to level it.

The moisture content of freshly cut slabs can be really high, too high to use for projects. The thicker the material, the longer it takes to dry. If the slab isn't dry when you start working with it, it can warp, twist, or crack over the course of the project. The door is open for lots of problems with wood that has not reached equilibrium. Checking the MC (moisture content) before you start using a slab, **Photo 1**, is cheap insurance, and a must-do. Wood should be at an MC of 6 – 12% to be considered project ready. Check how deeply your moisture meter reads. Many only read ¾" deep, or so. If that's the case, be sure to check thick slabs from both faces. If the wood is too wet to use, the simplest thing to do is set it aside and allow the wood to dry.

3. Place your slab on a large, flat surface to check for twist. If two corners are touching and two corners aren't, you've got a twist to deal with.

Slabs are rarely perfectly flat and may also be rough sawn from the sawmill. You'll need to flatten and clean up the slab before you can use it on a project. A straightedge will show you if a slab isn't flat, **Photo 2**. Place the slab on a flat surface (the floor works) to check for twist, **Photo 3**. If it rocks or you can see that two corners touch and two don't, the slab has a twist in it. Even if the piece will fit through your planer, it's best to flatten one face first. Planers by themselves aren't good at removing twist.

4. Measure from the bench to the top of the slab on opposite corners on a twisted slab and use shims to make the measurements the same. T-track in the work surface provides a way to secure the slab.

5. This shop-made leveling jig is easy to make, and uses 2x4s for the rails. The gantry helps locate the rails on the work surface.

6. The gantry bridges from rail to rail, providing a platform for your router to ride on.

Flattening with a Router

A hand-held router can be used, in conjunction with a jig, to flatten your slabs. You'll need a work surface large enough for the slab to fit on, and a way to secure the slab to the surface. A large workbench is great for this, but plywood on sawhorses can also work. This approach works well for both face grain and end grain slabs.

If the slab is twisted use shims to take the rock out of it, **Photo 4**, ensuring the measurements on opposing corners are the same. This minimizes the amount of material you'll need to remove, leaving the slab as thick as possible. Simply slide a shim into the gap under each corner, measure the gap, and adjust the shims as necessary to make the two gap measurements match. Be careful to not push the shims so far under these corners that you lift the two corners that were in contact with your bench. When you have the shims correctly positioned add a bit of hot glue between the shims and the slab to make sure the shims stay in place.

This shop-made set up is low-tech and easy to make but doesn't provide dust collection. It consists of a gantry made from plywood for your router to ride on and rails for the gantry to ride on. Clamp two straight 2x4s to your work surface, **Photo 5**, to serve as rails. If a slab is especially thick you can use 2x6s instead or, for thin slabs, you can rip the 2x4s to a narrower width. The clamps holding the rails in place also prevent the router gantry from falling off the ends of the rails.

The gantry is made from two guides connected by bridges on each end. The router guides, **Photo 6**, are made from four ¾" x 2" plywood strips. The strips need to be long enough to span the work surface and rest on top of the rails. The router guides shown here are 48" long. It's handy to make two gantries, one for wide slabs and one for narrow slabs.

Fasten the plywood strips together with glue and screws to create two L-shaped guides. Span the router guides with a bridge that establishes the spread between the L-shaped pieces and acts as a stop for the router, **Photo 7**. Make the bridges ¹⁄₁₆" longer than the diameter of your router base.

The router should easily move along the guides, but not be sloppy. Clamp the bridge in place and test the fit of the router before gluing and screwing the bridges into place. In addition to establishing the spread, the bridge prevents the router bit from accidentally contacting the rails. Add a ¾" x 1½" retainer, **Photo 8**, to the bottom of guides, to keep the gantry from sliding off the rails.

You can use nearly any flat bottom router bit to flatten slabs, **Photo 9**, but a large diameter bit will do the work faster than a small diameter bit. A 2" or larger bit is ideal for this work. A 12-amp (2.25 HP) variable speed router is a great choice for this work, providing ample power AND the variable speed required for large diameter bits, which require slower speeds to operate properly. Make sure to reference the manufacturer's recommendation for operating speed. Since the router is sitting on the rails and on top of the gantry, it's fairly high above the work. A router collet extension is often required to give the bit enough reach to get to the slab.

7. Bridge the L-shaped router guides with a ¾" x 2" piece. This piece sets the distance between the router guides, and acts as a stop.

8. Fasten a piece to the bottom of the gantry. This acts as a retainer that prevents the gantry from sliding off the rails.

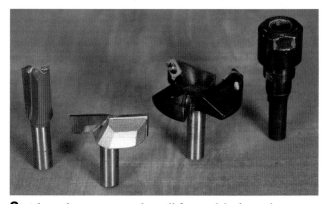

9. A large diameter router bit will flatten slabs faster than a small diameter bit. A collet extension, right, is typically necessary to get the bit far enough beyond the router base.

10. Flatten the slab by making multiple passes across its face, increasing the depth of cut slightly with each pass.

11. When you've machined the top face flat you can either plane the other face or flip the slab and repeat the flattening process using your router.

12. Commercially made systems, like the Slab Flattening Mill from Woodpeckers, offer the advantage of dust collection.

With the router jig complete, you're ready to flatten a slab, **Photo 10**. Be sure to wear appropriate safety gear, including safety glasses, hearing protection, and a dust mask. Start by removing about 1/16" per pass. When you set the depth for the first pass be sure you're setting it at the highest spot on the slab. Soft woods may allow deeper cuts. Listen to the router, and don't overwork it. Slide the router on the gantry, moving it across the slab. Reposition the gantry and make another pass. Move the gantry by half the diameter of the router bit each time, allowing each pass to overlap the previous pass. Continue increasing depth of cut and making passes until the top face is flat, **Photo 11**. If the slab will fit in your planer you can now place the flat face down on your planer bed and machine the other face until it's also flat and parallel to the first face. Otherwise flip the slab over and repeat the flattening process on the opposite face.

If you'd prefer to buy, instead of build, your slab flattening jig, commercially made systems are available, **Photo 12**. The approach is the same but with metal components instead of wood, which can give you a flatter slab because there's less flex in the gantry. The biggest gain from using a commercially made system, though, is integrated dust collection ports, which you can hook to a shop vacuum or dust collector. This is a huge advantage of commercial jigs, since this process creates a lot of dust.

13. Follow up the router work with sanding to remove marks left by the router bit.

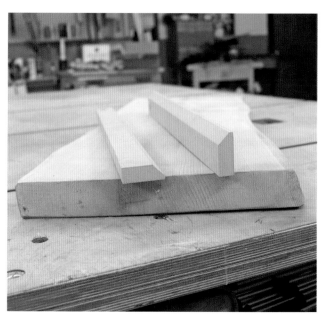

14. Winding sticks can be used to find twist and high spots in your slabs. These are made out of ¾"MDF.

Regardless of which system you use, your slab will have tracks on it left behind by the router bit. Sand the slab, **Photo 13**, to remove those marks. Start with a belt sander, if you have one, equipped with 80-grit sandpaper, and progress to a random orbit sander. Sand to 120-grit at this stage, leaving finish sanding until the project is further along.

Flattening with Winding Sticks

An alternative to flattening with a router-based jig is using winding sticks coupled with a power plane, hand plane or belt sander. This process works great on narrower slabs that will fit through your planer and is better for face grain slabs than end grain slabs. End grain slabs should never be sent through a planer. The planer knives can catch on the end grain and cause the slab to blow apart.

Winding sticks, **Photo 14**, are very simple. Use a stable material – the sticks are no good if they don't remain straight. Make them 2" wide and as long as you need for your projects. Cut a 45-degree angle on

one edge, leaving a ¼" wide flat on the top edge. The distinct top edge is the focal line for sighting over the winding sticks.

With the sticks on your slab, crouch down to eye level with the top of the sticks, **Photo 15**. If the slab is twisted or has high spots, like a crown, the edges

15. Place the winding sticks on your slab and get in a position where you can sight across the edges.

of the sticks will be out of parallel, **Photo 16**. The high end of the stick indicates a high spot on the board. Mark those spots, **Photo 17**. Move the winding sticks to various locations and repeat the process. It's likely the slab has more than two high spots.

Eliminate the high spots by planing or sanding, **Photo 18**. Do light passes and frequently check your progress with the winding sticks so you don't turn the high spots into low spots.

16. Winding sticks on a twisted slab will look like this, out of alignment with each other.

17. Remove the winding sticks and mark the high spots.

18. Plane or sand the high spots down. Do frequent checks with the winding sticks.

You goal is to see parallel edges on the winding sticks along the whole length of the board, **Photo 19**. Check the slab in a number of spots to make sure it's completely flat.

With one flat face, the slab is ready for your planer. Plane it with the flat face down on the planer bed. Your planer will make the other face flat, and parallel to the face you worked on. When the second face is flat flip the board and use the planer to remove any planing or sanding marks on the first face.

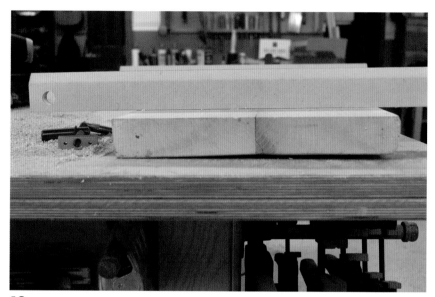

19. When the slab is flat the knife edges of the winding sticks will be parallel to each other.

20. If bark remains on the edges give it a tug test. See if you can flake it off with your hands.

21. Use a draw knife to remove loose bark, or to slice off bark that you want to eliminate.

Treating Edges

The whole appeal of live edge slabs is the look that the organic edges provide. As part of the drying and milling process, sometimes the bark remains attached, sometimes it's loose, sometimes it has already fallen off. Check remaining bark by tugging on it, **Photo 20**. If it's still firmly attached at this point, it should be sound enough to leave on the slab and you can count on it staying stuck. If the bark is questionable or you simply want to remove it for aesthetics, use a draw knife to slice it from the edge, **Photo 21**. Take light cuts with the draw knife and be careful to not cut the remaining live edge.

A live edge should look like a live edge. The slab shouldn't get all of the cool, natural contours sanded out of it, but it does need to be pleasant to touch. A mop sander, **Photo 22**, is a great tool for this. The sanding head is made up of fingers of sandpaper, similar to a buffing wheel. Mount the mop sander (also called a flutter sander) in a drill and press it against the edge, **Photo 23**. It's gentle enough that it won't remove lots of material, but it will knock off any loose pieces and leave a smooth surface behind.

22. A mop sander works great for cleaning up and smoothing live edges.

23. Use the mop sander in a drill and run it against the edge of the slab to remove loose pieces and knock down sharp edges.

Epoxy and Slabs

The prettiest slabs are the ones that have the most character. What some people might consider defects — holes, splits, bark inclusions, knots — can also be seen as characteristics that make a piece of wood unique and beautiful. It's great to embrace these characteristics, but not always practical. Holes and cracks aren't a great addition to a tabletop. This is where epoxy comes in. It can be a handy problem solver and, like choosing a stain color, can also add beautiful accents.

This chapter isn't intended to give you an all-encompassing knowledge of working with epoxy. Instead, it's presented as an overview of epoxy's capabilities and how it can help you with your projects, along with some tips for working with epoxy. The most important thing with epoxy, as with many things, is to read the manufacturer's instructions for the product and follow them to a T. Epoxy is expensive, so you don't want to waste it.

There are lots of epoxy products available, **Photo 1**. It's very important to choose the right epoxy for what you're doing. The product used for filling a deep crack or hole is different from the product used for putting a thin layer on top of a piece of wood. Using the wrong product can be bad. Epoxy is exothermic, meaning it gives off heat as it cures. Doing a deep pour with an epoxy that was developed to be used as a thin layer on a tabletop will result in LOTS of heat and a very poor epoxy finish.

Adding Color

Epoxy is clear, but it doesn't have to stay that way. Adding pigment to epoxy, **Photo 2**, gives it a single tone or color, **Photo 3**. Adding a small amount of pigment will give the epoxy color but leave it translucent. Additional pigment will make the epoxy opaque. Pigment is very concentrated. It's best to start by adding a small amount, mixing the pigment in, and checking the results. Pour a small amount on a piece of scrap to see if you're getting the opacity you want. You can always add more.

Mica powder, **Photo 4**, also gives epoxy color, but it's more pearlescent, **Photo 5**. An array of colors can be poured on a project and mixed in place to blend them together. Epoxy tinted with only mica powder tends to be translucent. You can mix and match types of colorant. Add blue pigment to a blue mica powder mix to give it more opacity. Coloring epoxy is more art than science. It's very important to experiment on a small scale before trying this on a large project.

1. Some epoxies are designed to be used to fill deep pockets, others are meant only for thin layers. Using the correct product is critical.

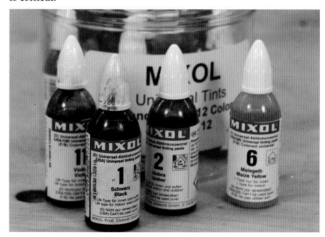

2. Mix pigment into epoxy to give it color. Pigment is very concentrated. A drop or two goes a long way.

3. Pigment provides a single, uniform color for your project.

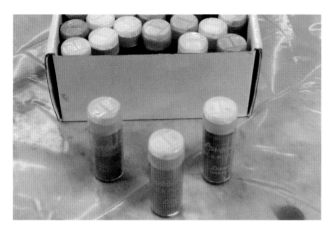

4. Mica powder, also an ingredient of soap and makeup, provides color and shimmer.

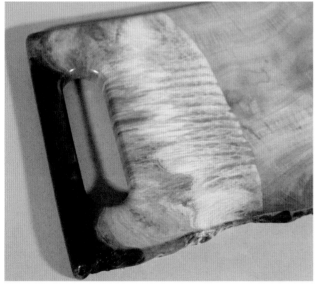

5. The colors produced by mica powder have a pearlescence. Pigment and mica powder can be used together.

6. This is a beautiful piece of live edge walnut, but it has a large void and a significant end crack.

7. If the holes on the front go all the way through the board they'll need to be dammed on the back side.

Filling Large Voids

If you've found a lovely slab you want to use as a desk or tabletop, but it has large holes in it from knots, cracks or other inclusions, **Photo 6**, epoxy will provide the level surface you need. Check the back of the board to see if the voids go all the way through, **Photo 7**. If they do, you'll need to seal the holes in the back. If there's any chance of a leak, even if the crack or hole looks tiny, take the time to seal it so you don't end up with an epoxy drip (or worse, having all the epoxy leak out while you're waiting for it to cure).

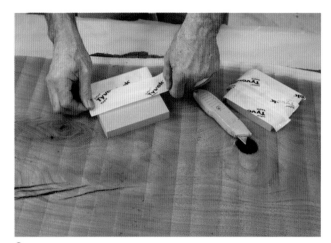

8. Make the dams from scrap and cover them with house wrap tape.

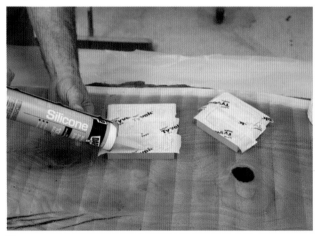

9. Apply a bead of 100% silicone caulk around the perimeter of each dam.

10. Put the dams in place, making sure you've completely covered the holes.

Use scrap to make the dams to contain epoxy, cutting them about 2" larger than the spot you're trying to seal. Cover the dams with house wrap tape, **Photo 8**, to prevent the epoxy from sticking to them. Silicone caulk acts as an adhesive and gasket so you can fasten the dams to the back of the slab. Put a bead of caulk on each dam, **Photo 9**, making sure it's continuous, leaving no gaps for the epoxy to find its way through. Place the dams over the holes, **Photo 10**, and allow the silicone to dry over night before pouring the epoxy.

Epoxy Prep

Prep the area where you'll be pouring epoxy by covering your work surface with 6-mil plastic sheeting. Epoxy won't stick to the plastic, so you'll have easy drip clean up later. Also, check the ambient room temperature where you'll be working. Most manufacturers recommend a room temperature of at least 68 degrees. It's important to follow this rule to get the epoxy to work and flow correctly. The epoxy should also be warm, so make sure it's in the heated space at least a day before you plan on using it. Put your slab up on blocks. That way if there's a little bit of epoxy overflow it'll just drip on the plastic instead of puddling between the slab and the plastic (meaning you'll have to sand it off later).

Level the slab, **Photo 11**, by checking it side to side and end to end. Put shims under it, where needed, to keep it level. Epoxy, like water, will find its own level. The larger the piece you're working on, the more critical leveling the slab becomes. If you neglect to level the slab you may end up with epoxy that's even with the top of the slab in one spot, and way below it in another.

11. It's very important to level the slab to make sure the epoxy pours at the same level everywhere on the slab.

12. Measure the void and calculate how many cubic inches it is to determine how many ounces of epoxy you need to fill it.

13. Use an air compressor to blow stray dust and chips out.

14. Create a berm around the void with a hot glue gun or caulk. This allows you to slightly overfill the void. Place the berm ¼"—½" outside the void.

Calculate how much epoxy you need by measuring the length, width and depth of the void, **Photo 12**, and multiplying those numbers to get cubic inches. For instance, a 2" x 18" hole in a 1¾" thick slab is 63 cubic inches. Multiply cubic inches by .55 to convert to ounces. Since most voids in wood aren't uniform rectangles, you'll need to do some estimating. It's better to mix a little too much than not enough, especially when you're mixing with color. It can be difficult to mix a second batch of color that's an exact match.

Use an air compressor to clean out the void, **Photo 13**, so random particulates don't float up in the epoxy later, and a hot glue gun to create a berm around the void, **Photo 14**. The berm lets you pour epoxy higher than the top face of the slab. This is handy on large voids because the epoxy may slowly seep into the grain and, without a slight overpour, end up lower than the surface of the slab.

It can take a long time for the epoxy to completely settle into every fissure in the wood. Without a berm around the void, you'd need to babysit the epoxy, watching it to see if you need to add more. A berm lets you pour epoxy and leave it alone, though it's not a bad idea to peek at the pour periodically over the first few hours to make certain that, even with the berm, it hasn't settled below the surface of the slab. The berm can also be made with 100% silicone caulk, but that would have to be allowed to dry overnight before you pour epoxy. You can pour within a hot glue berm as soon as the glue cools off.

Mix and Pour

Before working with epoxy, get your safety gear ready — safety glasses, rubber gloves and a VOC (volatile organic compounds) mask if you don't have good ventilation in your workspace. Read the manufacturer's instructions when you're ready to mix and pour the epoxy. The resin and hardener need to be mixed in specific proportions, provided by the manufacturer, and for a specific period of time. Don't take any shortcuts on this.

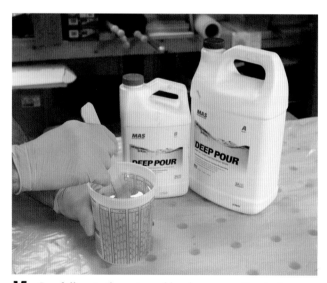

15. Carefully mix the resin and hardener according to the manufacturer's instructions.

16. Pour the mixed epoxy into the voids.

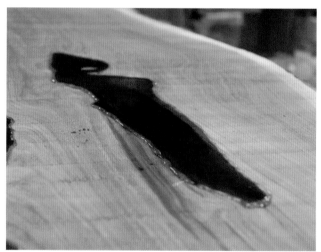

17. Fill the voids to the top of the berm. Monitor the epoxy for an hour or so to see if you need to add more.

Use a graduated mixing cup, **Photo 15**, measure carefully, and thoroughly mix the two parts. Some epoxies are mixed by weight, not by volume. Read the instructions. Don't be too aggressive when you're mixing, or you'll put a lot of air bubbles into the epoxy. When using deep pour epoxy, it's a good idea to let the mixture sit for 20 minutes before doing the pour to allow bubbles to rise out of it. When it's ready, pour the epoxy into the voids, **Photo 16**, filling them to the top of the hot glue berms, **Photo 17**. It's not impossible that you'll need to add more epoxy as the liquid flows into the slab's nooks and crannies. A heat gun is sometimes used on epoxy to remove bubbles, but usually isn't needed for deep pours. Deep pour formulas typically cure very slowly, which allow the bubbles to exit on their own.

Clean Up the Slab

Many epoxies are hard to the touch after about 24 hours but take much longer than that, up to a week, to be fully cured. Cure time is included in the manufacturer's instructions. When the epoxy is cured remove the dams from the back of the slab by tapping a chisel between the dam and the slab, **Photo 18**. The dam will easily release. Use a sharp chisel to remove excess silicone from the slab, **Photo 19**. A sander will remove the silicone, too, but may quickly clog the abrasive.

Both faces of the slab need to be sanded to remove excess epoxy. Because of the hot glue berm used on top of the slab, the epoxy on the top face will be quite a bit higher than the surrounding wood. The back side will be closer to flush. Sand both sides until the epoxy is even with the slab, **Photo 20**, starting with 80-grit sandpaper. A belt sander will be the fastest way to do this, but a random orbit sander will also work.

18. Remove the dams after the epoxy is fully cured.

19. Slice the excess silicone off the back of the slab to prevent it from clogging up your sandpaper.

20. Sand the epoxy until it's flush with the wood.

21. Use a random orbit sander to finish sand the epoxy and slab.

After the epoxy is sanded flush, use a random orbit sander on the epoxy and surrounding wood, **Photo 21**, sanding it to 220-grit. When the sanding is complete apply finish to the entire slab, including over the epoxy. For many brands of epoxy, sanding beyond 220-grit can make it difficult for finish to adhere. Check the instructions for your epoxy for specific sanding and finishing recommendations. All this work is worth it though, for the finished result: a beautiful, perfectly level slab, **Photo 22**.

22. The surface of the slab is now perfectly flat, and flaws have become features. Clear epoxy allows you to see through the void.

Fill Cracks with Color

23. Cracks and small holes in a slab add character, but don't make for a good work surface.

24. Prevent epoxy leaks by sealing small cracks in the back of the slab with HVAC tape.

There's nothing wrong with having cracks in the slabs you're using for your projects, **Photo 23**, unless you want a dead flat surface. Finish won't fill the cracks, but epoxy will. You'll need to seal the back of the slab to prevent leaks. Small cracks, up to ⅛" wide, can be sealed with aluminum HVAC tape instead of dams, **Photo 24**. Apply tape to anything that looks even remotely like it could leak. After the tape has been applied, press it firmly in place with your hand to make sure it's completely sealed against the slab. The wood needs to be smooth in

25. Mix the epoxy and add pigment, mica powder, or both.

26. Fill the cracks with your colored epoxy.

order for the tape to stick. If you do this step after flattening the slab with your router, it'll be smooth enough. If the slab still has marks from the sawmill, the tape probably won't stick well enough to work.

Small cracks can often be filled with a tabletop formula epoxy instead of a deep pour epoxy. Before doing this double-check your epoxy to make sure the volume of epoxy the crack requires isn't beyond what the table top formula can handle. Calculate the amount of epoxy you need and mix the epoxy according to its instructions and add color, **Photo 25.** You can use a color that blends in, like using black or brown with a walnut slab, or go in a completely different direction and use a color that will stand out as an accent of its own.

After mixing the epoxy, pour it into the cracks, **Photo 26.** It's difficult to use berms on pours like this because the cracks are often spread over such a wide area. Instead, use a squeegee to move the epoxy across the surface and push it into the cracks until they're full, **Photo 27.** Let the epoxy settle for a while and check to see if you need to add more. If you see bubbles use a heat gun to gently blow warm air over the wet epoxy surface, and the bubbles will come right out. Sand and finish the slab after the epoxy is cured to achieve an amazing, accented surface, **Photo 28.**

27. Use a squeegee to push the epoxy into the cracks.

28. The filled cracks add a beautiful accent to the slab.

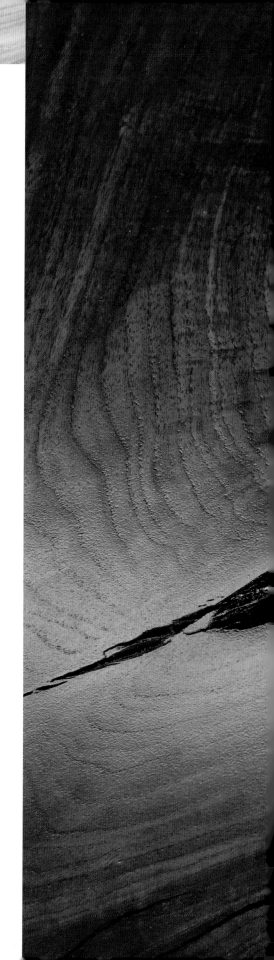

Cutting In Bowties

Bowties can be used to hold cracks together, mask defects, or simply act as a decorative element. Using contrasting species of wood will make the bowtie inlay really pop. Here's a look at three approaches to adding bowties to your slabs. The words bowtie and butterfly are often used interchangeably in this context (though we'll stick to bowtie here). When this process is used to hide a defect, the result is often called a Dutchman. The same techniques used to install bowties can be used with a variety of different shaped inlays.

Rules of the Road

Many woodworkers use bowties to span cracks. The expectation shouldn't be that the bowtie will prevent the crack from getting larger. Once your slab is dry and stable, existing cracks should remain the same and new cracks shouldn't be forming. But cracks may weaken the slab and a bowtie will act like a bridge, tying the two sides together to help stabilize the slab.

If you're relying on a bowtie to stabilize a crack, a good rule of the thumb is for the thickness of the bowtie to be ⅓ the thickness of the slab. Keep this in mind as you're choosing which method you'll use to make the bowtie, since some methods limit the thickness of the bowtie. If the bowtie is purely decorative, though, it doesn't matter how thick it is.

The size of the bowtie is largely aesthetic, but it can also be based on the size of the crack you're spanning or defect you're covering. When you're spanning a crack, make sure that more than half of each wing is embedded in the wood. If the bowtie is 3" long, each side is 1½", so at least ¾" of each side should be surrounded by wood.

When using a bowtie to mask a defect, like a knot, determine if you want the defect completely covered, or if you want some of it to show, and size the bowtie accordingly.

Making Bowties from Scratch

Making your bowties from scratch, as opposed to using a commercially made template, gives you complete control over the dimensions. Lay out the bowties so they're twice as long as they are wide at the widest point, and make the wings at 12-degree angles. 12-degrees provides a time-tested angle that is neither too steep or too shallow for an effective dovetail. Whether you're laying bowties out on paper or on wood, the approach is the same. The easiest way to lay out the 12-degree angle is by using a piece of scrap cut to that angle, **Photo 1**. Mark out a rectangle that defines the outside dimensions of the bowtie, **Photo 2**. Align the edge and corner of the

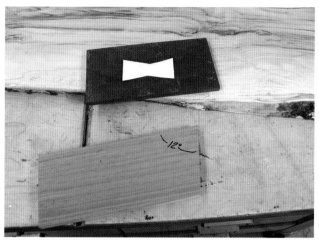

1. Make a bowtie layout tool by cutting a piece of scrap at 12-degrees using a miter saw or table saw.

2. Lay out a rectangle using the width and length dimensions of the bowtie.

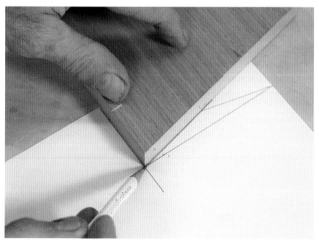

3. Use the board you cut at 12-degrees to lay out the shape on some paper.

4. This provides the layout you need for a bowtie.

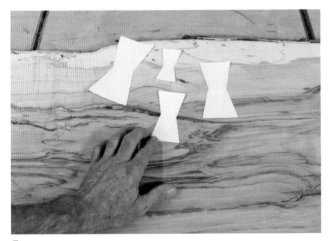

5. Experiment with different sizes of paper bowties to determine what size or sizes you need for your project.

6. You can create a "zipper" by using multiple bowties, graduating their sizes.

piece you cut at 12-degrees with the end and corner of the rectangle and draw four angled lines, **Photo 3**, to get a bowtie, **Photo 4**.

Decide what size bowtie you need for your project by cutting a variety of sizes from paper and laying them on your workpiece, **Photo 5**. You may want to use more than one bowtie on long cracks, and multiple bowties don't have to be the same size, **Photo 6**. Some people call this look a bowtie zipper.

Once you know what size and how many bowties you need, lay them out on the bowtie material. The grain should run end to end on the bowtie (the same direction as the long dimension). Cut the bowtie to shape, **Photo 7**, staying outside the lines. Use a sharp chisel to remove the saw marks and trim the

7. Cut the bowtie using a bandsaw, handsaw, or jigsaw. Stay outside your layout lines.

four edges down to the pencil lines, **Photo 8**. Make very light passes, holding the back of the chisel flat against the edge as you cut. It's important to keep the edges perpendicular to the face. Take your time, always working downhill from the wide to the narrow part of the bowtie. Use a straight edge or the edge of your chisel to check the edge of the bowtie and make sure it's straight, **Photo 9**. Practice this technique on scrap before trying it on project material. The edges of the bowtie need to be straight, but since it gets traced onto the slab, small variations can be accommodated.

Apply double-faced tape to the back of the bowtie and position it on the slab, **Photo 10**. Tape guarantees that it doesn't slip while you're tracing it. The best tool for tracing the edges of the bowtie is a marking knife, **Photo 11**. This makes a very precise line, which is important for getting a good fit between the bowtie and the pocket in the slab. If you do use a pencil keep it needle sharp by rolling it across 180-grit sandpaper, **Photo 12**. Make sure the marking knife or pencil is tight against the bowtie as you trace it, so you have a precise shape to follow, **Photo 13**.

8. Use a chisel, cutting downhill, to pare the edges down to the pencil lines.

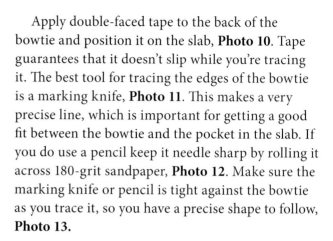

10. Stick the bowtie in place using double-faced tape.

9. Use the edge of your chisel to make sure the surface is straight.

11. Use a marking knife to trace the bowtie onto the slab.

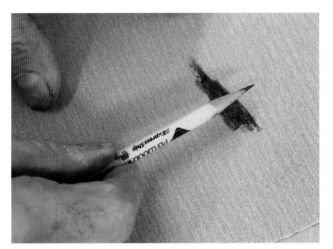

12. If you trace the bowtie using a pencil, make sure it's very sharp.

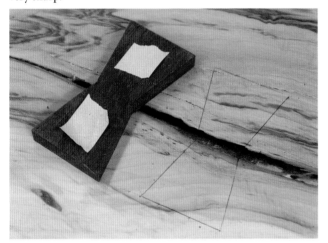

13. Careful tracing provides an accurate outline.

The pocket cut can be done with a fixed base or plunge base router. Install a ¼" router bit in your router and set the depth of cut, **Photo 14**. On small bowties, 1" wide or less, use a ⅛" diameter router bit. Set the depth of cut to slightly less than the thickness of the bowtie. Give the router bit a starting point in the pocket by drilling a hole, **Photo 15**. Use masking tape or a stop collar on the bit to set the depth of the hole, making it the same as the depth you set the router bit to.

The pocket for the bowtie is routed freehand. Get in a good position where you can look into the base of the router and see the router bit, **Photo 16**. Let the

14. Set the depth of cut on the router to ¹⁄₃₂" less than the thickness of the bowtie.

15. Drill a hole inside the pocket layout so there's a place for the router bit to start.

16. Freehand rout the pocket. Practice on scrap before doing this on a project.

heels of your hands rest on the slab so you're moving the router with your fingers, not your arms. Your fingers are better at small, precise movements. Start in the center of the pocket and make progressively larger circles, working toward the layout lines. Stay $\frac{1}{16}$" away from the lines, **Photo 17**. The closer to the lines you're able to cut, **Photo 18**, the easier the chisel work will be. But it's important to not go beyond the layout lines. If you do, make a larger bowtie and repeat the process.

Finalize the fit of the bowtie by paring the walls of the pocket with a sharp chisel, **Photo 19**. This can typically be done without using a mallet if the chisel is sharp and you make the cuts correctly. The slab should be about waist height so you can lean over it. Lock your arm and shoulder so that, as you lean forward, your upper body is putting pressure on the chisel, **Photo 20**, allowing you to cut a sliver from the pocket wall. This provides really good control over how much material you're removing, but use a mallet as needed if this technique isn't working for you. Be careful to keep the chisel and walls of the pocket perpendicular to the surface of the slab.

The bowtie will be easier to slip into the pocket if you cut a chamfer on all the back corners, **Photo 21**. Check the fit of the bowtie frequently, tapping it

17. Remove the waste from the center of the pocket and slowly work your way toward the layout lines.

19. Pare the sides of the pocket with a sharp chisel, working toward the layout lines.

18. A well-cut pocket is easy to clean up with a chisel.

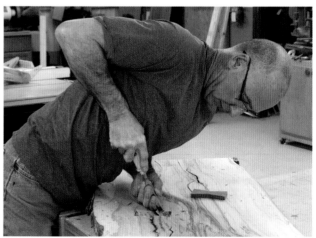

20. Lock your elbow and shoulder so you can lean against the chisel to pare out the waste.

21. Cut a chamfer on the back corners of the bowtie to make it easier to insert.

22. Stop and check the fit often. Don't tap the bowtie in too far or it will be impossible to remove.

gently into the pocket, **Photo 22**. Because the bowtie was cut and pared to shape freehand there will be one distinct way it will fit into the pocket. As you test the fit be sure to double-check and make sure you're inserting the bowtie in the correct orientation.

When you've achieved a good fit apply glue in the bottom of the pocket, **Photo 23**, and tap the bowtie in, **Photo 24**. A piece of scrap prevents the mallet from leaving dents in the bowtie, and also distributes the force of the mallet strikes so you don't crack the bowtie. Allow the glue to dry, sand the bowtie flush, **Photo 25**, and admire your work, **Photo 26**.

23. Brush glue in the bottom of the pocket.

24. Tap the bowtie in, protecting it with a piece of scrap.

25. Sand the bowtie flush with the surface of the slab.

26. A well-fitted bowtie provides a beautiful addition to your work.

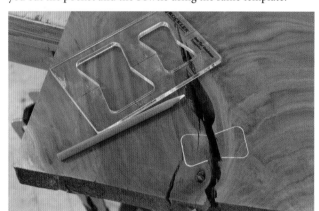

27. Commercially made template kits like this one rely on a two-piece guide bushing. A removable ring on the bushing lets you cut the pocket and the bowtie using the same template.

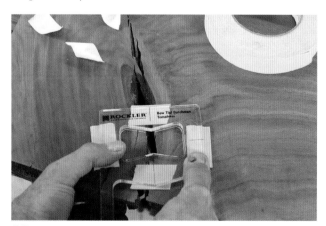

28. Experiment with bowtie size and position by tracing the template onto your slab.

29. Use double-faced tape to secure the template to your workpiece.

Template Cut Pocket and Bowties

A number of companies sell kits that can be used to cut both the pocket and the bowtie, **Photo 27**. These kits must be used with a plunge router and the two-piece guide bushing that comes with the kit, so make sure your router base can accommodate the bushing. The guide bushing mounted in the router base prevents the router bit from contacting the template. Maximum bowtie thickness with these kits is typically around ⅜".

The kits come with complete instructions, but here are a few tips that will help you succeed when using them. You can get a feel for your options with the template by tracing it onto the slab, **Photo 28**, to see how the bowtie will look. Because of the guide bushing, the final bowtie is slightly smaller than the shape provided by the template. A white charcoal pencil, available at art stores, is great for marking on dark wood.

Practice using the kit on scrap before using it on one of your projects. Cut the pocket first, because the pocket is easier to cut than the bowtie. Hold the

30. Position the router on the template with the guide bushing inside the template, plunge into the wood and move the router inside the template to remove the waste.

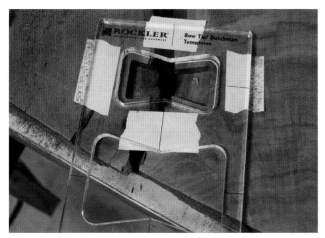

31. Check your work before removing the template and re-cut as needed.

32. Use double-faced tape to to secure the bowtie material to scrap, and the template to the bowtie material.

33. Carefully position the router and plunge into the material.

template in place with double-face tape, **Photo 29**. The router bit's depth of cut should be slightly less than the thickness of the bowtie. Cut the pocket in ⅛" deep increments to prevent breaking the router bit. Follow the instructions for setting up the guide bushing, position your router on the template and plunge the bit into the wood, **Photo 30**. Move your router within the template to remove the waste, traversing the entire template area. Dust and chips will build up in the template. Stop frequently to clear the waste out of the cut or it will interfere with the guide bushing riding against the template (which will prevent a good fit). Make a final pass moving clockwise around the inside of the template.

Be sure to double check your work, **Photo 31**, prior to removing the template. Make sure the bottom of the pocket is completely flat. If there are high spots, as shown here, it's easy to clean them up with the router, as long as the template is still secure. Check the edge of the pocket relative to the template edges. They should be parallel. You'll see high spots if the guide bushing moved away from the template as you were cutting. Make any necessary corrections and remove the template.

Secure the bowtie material and template, **Photo 32**, and follow the kit instructions for the guide bushing. The bowtie material should be planed to finished thickness before you start cutting. It's important to have scrap below the bowtie material because the cut goes all the way through. Set the depth of cut to allow the router bit to cut ¹⁄₃₂" deeper than the thickness of the bowtie. Place the router on the template with the guide bushing tight against the template, **Photo 33**, and plunge into the bowtie material, cutting ⅛" deep per pass and moving clockwise. When routing the pocket, it doesn't matter where you make the plunge, since the entire interior is being removed. When making the bowtie the bushing must be tight against the template before plunging because you're making an exterior cut, **Photo 34**.

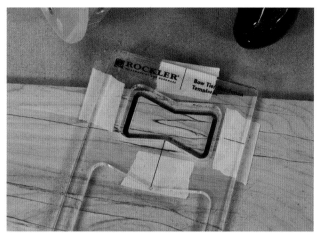

34. Be very careful when cutting the bowtie. If the guide bushing pulls away from the template, the bowtie is ruined.

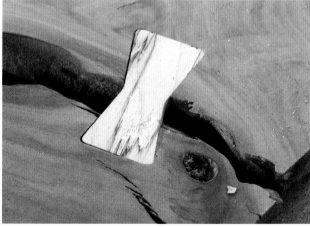

36. Small gaps like this, caused by the guide bushing pulling away from the template, can be easily fixed.

35. Glue and clamp the bowtie in place with wax paper between the caul and the bowtie.

Check the fit of the bowtie. You may find you need to remake bowties the first few times you use the kit, because it's easy for the guide bushing to pull away from the template on this cut. Apply glue in the pocket. If the bowtie is near the edge of the slab it can be clamped, **Photo 35.** Use a caul between the clamp and the bowtie to distribute the clamp pressure, and wax paper between the caul and the bowtie to prevent the caul from being glued to the surface if there's glue squeeze out.

37. Push yellow glue into the gaps using your finger.

38. Sand over the bowtie while the glue is still wet.

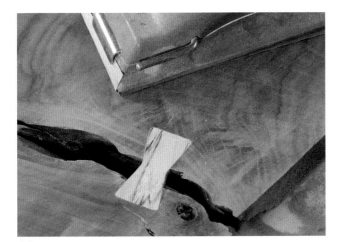

39. This is a great trick for hiding small gaps in your woodworking projects.

If there are small gaps between the bowtie and the pocket, **Photo 36**, fill them with yellow glue, **Photo 37**. Hand sand the bowtie while the glue is still wet, **Photo 38**, using 120-grit sandpaper. The sawdust and glue will mix, filling the crack with perfectly colored wood dough. We'll keep that secret to ourselves, and no one will ever know, **Photo 39**. Notice that bowties cut with these kits have rounded corners, not sharp corners.

Two-Tone Inlays

Another form of commercially made inlay kit, **Photo 40**, uses a guide bushing to cut the pocket. The bowties are premade, provided by the company. This creates lots of options for bowties, such as two-tone, metal, and many shapes beyond bowties. This style also results in bowties with sharp outside corners (with the aid of a little chisel work).

The routing process is very similar to the previous template kit, but this system doesn't require a plunge router because you're not cutting the bowtie. After the pocket has been routed use a sharp chisel on the corners of the recess, **Photo 41**. Unlike the bowties made completely from scratch, a chisel is only used to clean up the corners. Glue the bowtie in place, **Photo 42**, allow the glue to dry, and sand it flush for a beautiful two-tone look, **Photo 43**.

Both of the commercially made systems mentioned here have many shapes besides bowties available, and in multiple sizes. Check online or at woodworking specialty stores for these products. When you're hiding defects, you can also rout a pocket and fill it with epoxy instead of installing a wooden inlay.

40. Commercially made kits like this one use a one-piece guide bushing, create bowties with sharp corners, and can be used for two-tone bowties.

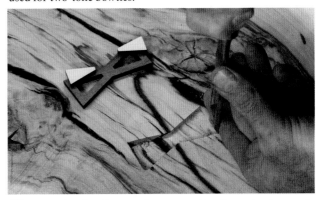

41. Use a chisel to sharpen the corners after the pocket is routed.

42. Glue in the two-piece bowtie.

43. Sand the bowtie flush.

Create a Waterfall Edge

Waterfall edges take advantage of mitered corners to create continuous grain that, like a waterfall, flows from the horizontal surface to the vertical surface. Table legs are a very common application for waterfall edges, but you can use this technique any time two surfaces are coming together at a right angle.

Choose Your Material

1. Slabs used for a waterfall project have to be long enough to make all the parts the project requires, such as the legs and the top.

The slab you use for a waterfall project needs to be long enough to produce all the required parts, **Photo 1**. For instance, a 16" tall coffee table that's 48" long with two waterfall legs requires a slab that's over 80" long. Keep in mind that you can choose to do a waterfall on only one end and use another approach, like commercially made legs, for the other end.

Lay Out the Waterfall Cut

Live edge slabs typically don't have straight edges you can put a square against, so you need to create a reference line you can use to lay out the cuts required for the waterfall edge. Do this by creating a centerline axis on your slab. Working on the waterfall end of the slab (both ends if you're cutting legs on both ends of the slab), measure and mark the center of the slab in two places, **Photo 2**. Connect the two center lines, **Photo 3**, to create the axis line. Mark out the location of the miter cut on the axis line, **Photo 4**, using the length of the legs plus 1" to determine the location. The legs will be cut to their final length after the miter is cut.

2. Measure and mark the center of the slab in two spots.

3. Use a straightedge and draw a line from center line to center line.

4. Mark the location of the miter based on the length of the table legs, making it at least 1" longer than the legs.

5. You now have the miter accurately located on the slab.

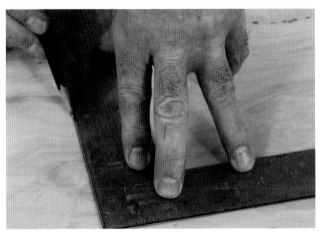

6. Put one leg of a square on the centerline axis and draw a line at the miter location.

7. Extend the line by positioning the square on the line you just made, and drawing it across the rest of the slab.

If you want a 16" tall table and are creating a waterfall edge on both ends, the miter cut is located at 17". If you're putting a waterfall edge at one end of the table and using a commercially made leg on the other end as shown here, add the thickness of the slab to the length of the leg, then add the extra 1" to determine the location of the miter cut. A framing square works well for marking out the miter cut lines.

Place one leg of the square on the centerline axis with its corner at the miter cut location and draw a line, **Photo 5**. Align the square with the line you just made and draw a new line across the width of the slab, **Photo 6**. This provides a cut line for the miter that's perpendicular to the centerline axis you created on the slab, **Photo 7**.

Cut the Miter

The easiest and best way to cut the miter required for a waterfall edge is by using a track saw. Track saws provide the precision that's required to have a good-looking, accurately cut miter when it's assembled. It's a very good idea to practice making the cuts on scrap before you make them on a project piece. This is definitely not a cut that can be made freehand.

Secure the slab so it can't move while you're cutting it. Position the track on the miter cut line, **Photo 8**, and clamp the track in place. The large portion of the slab is clamped to a workbench with the shorter portion, the leg, cantilevered off the bench. Support the leg so it can't fall to the floor as you're cutting the miter. Before making a cut, make sure your saw is accurately set at 45-degrees, **Photo 9**. Cut the miter, **Photo 10**.

8. Position the saw track on the layout line.

9. Set your saw to 45-degrees and double-check the angle.

10. Make the cut, keeping the saw moving smoothly forward across the slab.

Move the large portion of the slab out of the way and clamp the leg you just cut to your bench. Position the track on the miter, **Photo 11**, and clamp it in place. This is the most important step in creating a good waterfall edge. You'll achieve the best waterfall, the best flow of grain from horizontal to vertical, by removing as little material as possible. The track should be located at the point where the horizontal surface meets the angle so the kerf of the saw is in the angled portion, not removing any material from the horizontal portion. Make the cut, **Photo 12**, and be sure to keep the triangular offcut that results. You'll use this when you clamp the joint.

11. Carefully place the track on the miter cut on the leg, positioning it at the point where the angled cut meets the horizontal surface.

12. Cut the second miter, again keeping the saw smoothly moving forward throughout the cut.

Finalize the Leg Length

The leg or legs can now be cut to final length. If you're building with a commercially made leg use it to mark out the length of the waterfall leg. Align one end of the metal leg with the miter on the inside face of the wooden leg, and mark the location of the other end, **Photo 13**. Do this in two places. Align your saw track with the two layout lines and make the cut, **Photo 14**.

If you're using two waterfall legs, establish their final length by measuring and marking the leg length on the outside face of the leg. Measure from the long point of the miter to establish the distance from the top of the table or bench to the floor. Make two marks, align the track with these marks and make the cuts.

The benefit to cutting the leg (or legs) to length after the miter is complete is that this guarantees the foot of the leg is parallel to the miter, eliminating wobble in the finished table. Additionally, transferring the length of a commercially made leg to the mitered waterfall leg is the easiest way to ensure they're identical in length.

Reinforce the Miter

Mitered joints in any project are inherently weak. A mitered waterfall edge, especially in a table application, needs to be reinforced. This can be done with loose tenons like dowels, Dominoes, or biscuits.

Put the mitered pieces on your bench, miter to miter. Position #20 biscuits every 2" – 3" across the joint and mark their locations on both boards, **Photo 15**. Set up your biscuit joiner and, before making a cut, double check to make certain your set up is right and the cutter won't come out through the face of the workpiece.

13. Determine the final length of the waterfall leg by transferring the length of the metal leg to it.

14. Align the track with the layout lines and cut the leg to its final length.

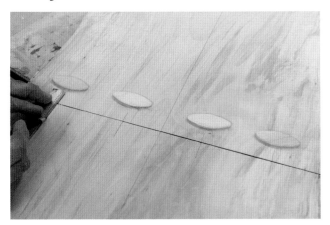

15. Locate biscuits every 2" to 3" across the miter and mark their locations on both boards.

16. Set your biscuit joiner to cut slots in the center of the miter cut, and make sure that at that position the cutter won't exit through the face of the workpiece.

17. Cut the biscuit slots in both halves of the joint.

With the biscuit joiner unplugged, position it past the edge of the workpiece and plunge the cutter to its maximum depth, **Photo 16**. Check the location of the cutter relative to the face of the workpiece. Change the fence location and move the slots as necessary. When you know the settings are right, cut the biscuit slots in your project pieces, **Photo 17**.

Create Feet

It isn't imperative to create feet on the legs, but feet can help prevent your project from wobbling. Very few floors are perfectly flat. If you leave the floor end of the leg straight it may rock on an imperfect floor. Feet also add a nice visual effect to the leg.

Here's a technique that results in a small arch between the feet. Divide the width of the leg by three, then divide that result by two to get the width of the feet. Lay the feet out on your leg and, if you're happy with the layout, clamp blocks on the layout lines, **Photo 18**. You can, of course, make the feet wider or narrower to get a different look. Create the arch by pressing a flexible ruler or thin piece of wood against the blocks and pushing to force it to

18. Mark out the locations for the feet and clamp blocks on the layout lines.

19. Create the arch by bowing a ruler or thin piece of wood against the blocks. Trace along the ruler.

20. Use double-faced tape or hot glue to secure the clamp blocks to the surface.

21. Apply masking tape on the inside face of the joint to prevent glue squeeze out from getting on the parts.

22. Brush glue onto the joint and inside the biscuit slots. Insert the biscuits and brush glue on them.

bow, **Photo 19**. Trace the ruler when you're happy with the curve. The arch on the leg shown here is 1" high. Cut the curve using a bandsaw or jigsaw, and sand it smooth.

Assemble the Miter Joint

Before applying any glue to the joint make sure you have everything you need — mallet, glue, glue brush, and clamps. You don't want to have to scurry around your shop looking for tools after you've started putting things together.

Grab the triangular offcut that was created when you cut the miter and cut it into clamping blocks that are 2" to 3" long. Secure the clamping blocks to each of the two parts of the miter joint with double-sided tape or hot-melt glue, **Photo 20**, positioning them about 3" apart and ¼" back from the edge. Wide slabs will need more clamping blocks than narrow slabs. The blocks allow you to get clamp pressure on the joint in line with the miter. If necessary, you can make more clamp blocks by ripping a 45-degree edge on scrap. Flip the parts over and apply masking tape to the inside faces, even with the edge of the miter cut, **Photo 21**.

Set your project up on your bench so you can assemble it. If you're using a metal leg on one end clamp it in place to hold that end up. Or use scrap blocking to hold the project up high enough that you can slip the legs under the miter. Rosin paper on your bench, available at home centers, protects it from glue.

Brush a uniform film of glue on the miter and inside the biscuit slots, **Photo 22**. Yellow glue works fine for these joints. Insert the biscuits and put glue on them. Brush glue onto the other part of the miter joint, and into the biscuit slots, **Photo 23**. Slip the joint together and remove the scrap that was supporting the project, **Photo 24**. As you're bringing the parts together pay attention to the grain pattern. Slide the parts back and forth to align the grain on the horizontal and vertical surfaces. Use a mallet, as needed, to tap the parts into alignment, **Photo 25**.

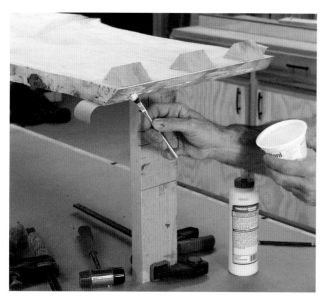

23. Brush glue on the other half of the joint and inside the slots. The end grain in miter joints soaks up a lot of glue, so it's important to put glue on both surfaces of the joint.

24. Bring the joint together and remove the temporary blocking.

Don't worry about the edges of the slabs aligning — that will be taken care of later. When the grain is correctly aligned place clamps on the clamp blocks and squeeze the joint closed, **Photo 26**.

After the glue has had ample drying time (I like to let the joint dry for a full 24 hours), use a mallet to gently knock the clamp blocks off the surface, **Photo 27**. If you used hot-melt glue to hold the clamp blocks on, you may need to use a heat gun to reactivate the glue so you can remove the blocks.

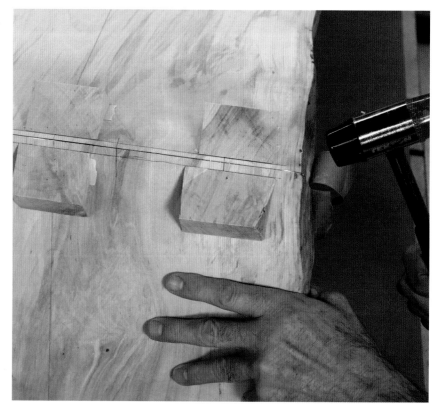

25. Use a mallet to tap the parts, bringing the horizontal and vertical grain into alignment with each other.

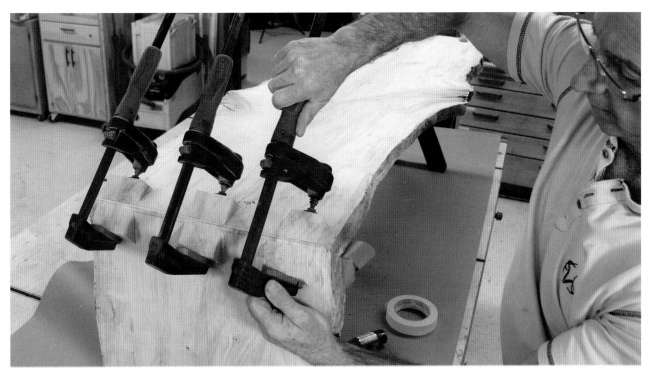

26. Put clamps on the clamp blocks and draw the joint closed.

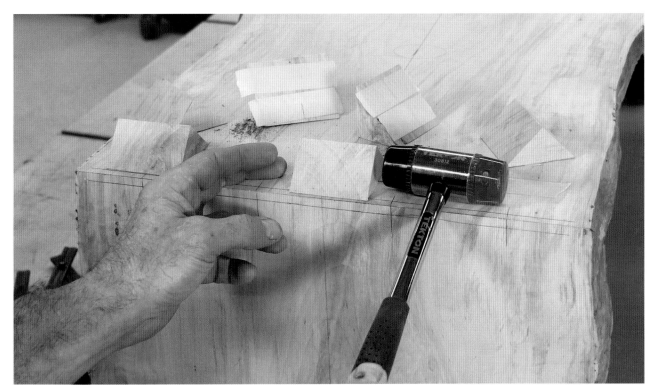

27. Allow the glue to dry. Use a mallet to rap the clamp blocks and free them from the surface.

Tweak the Miter Joint

You may need to do a few adjustments to your waterfall miter. Don't panic if there are small gaps visible in the joint, **Photo 28**. These can be easily fixed. Use your finger or a putty knife to push wood filler into the gaps, **Photo 29**. Tap the corner of the miter with a hammer while the filler is still wet, **Photo 30**. This peens the corner, pushing the wood fibers into the gap. Allow the filler to dry.

While the filler is drying have a look at the edges of the slab. They probably won't line up, **Photo 31**. This isn't the result of a mistake. It's because of the live edge and the miter. It's unlikely the organic shape of the live edge will align when the mitered parts are "folded" together. Sand the edges by hand with 180-grit sandpaper to blend them together, **Photo 32**.

28. Small gaps in the joint can be easily repaired.

30. Peen the corner of the miter with a hammer while the filler is still wet.

29. Use a wood filler that matches the color of your project material and pack it into gaps in the joint.

31. Check the edges of the slabs. They will probably be out of alignment.

When the filler is dry, sand the miter, **Photo 33**. Use fine paper and don't remove a lot of material. If you sand too much you may work your way past the filler and the peened fibers and expose a gap again. Hand sand the corner to gently round it, **Photo 34**.

Use fine grit sandpaper and, again, don't sand any more than you need to, or you may expose a new gap. This process will result in a very attractive miter joint and waterfall edge, **Photo 35**.

32. Hand sand the edges to make them flush with each other.

33. Sand the miter, being careful to not remove too much material and expose gaps.

34. Hand sand with fine paper to gently round the corner.

35. The result is a great looking waterfall edge.

Shop-made saw guide

A track saw is the best way to cut the miter joint required for a waterfall edge, but a shop-made saw guide for your circular saw isn't a bad second choice. Install a 60-tooth blade in your circular saw and measure from the blade to the edge of the saw's shoe, **Photo A**. Add 4" to this number and cut a piece of ¼" material to that width. A 32" long shop-made saw guide is very practical, but it can be made any length you need for your projects.

Glue a ¾" x 2" strip onto the ¼" material piece, **Photo B**. This 2" strip is the saw fence, and the saw will ride against it as you cut so it should be as straight as possible. After the glue is dry clamp the saw guide to a work surface and set your saw to 45-degrees. With the edge of the saw shoe riding against the fence cut through the base of the saw guide, **Photo C**. This results in a 45-degree cut in the base of the guide that will be used to locate the jig on your work.

Position the saw guide on the slab, aligning the bevel cut with the miter cut line, **Photo D**. Clamp the saw guide to the slab and make the cut, **Photo E**. Remove the jig, position it on the leg and clamp it in place. Cut the other half of the miter.

If you want to use a saw guide for square cuts in addition to mitered cuts, make a second jig and, with the saw set at 90-degrees, cut the ¼" base as described above.

A. Measure the distance from the blade to the edge of the shoe.

B. Glue and clamp the saw fence onto the ¼" thick base.

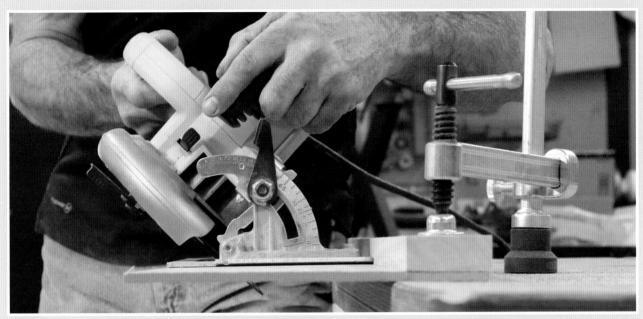

C. Position the saw shoe against the fence and cut through the ¼" base.

D. Use the bevel you cut to locate the saw guide on your workpiece, aligning the edge of the cut with your layout line.

E. Cut the miter joint following the same procedures outlined for use with a track saw

Finishes for Woodworking Projects

What finish to use for your woodworking project as well as how to apply that finish could be a book in and of itself. I'd definitely recommend you consult a few trusted resources on finishing. (My go-to is *Understanding Wood Finishing*, by Bob Flexner.) With that said, I'll share a few finishing methods with these slab projects in mind.

Food-Safe Finish

Nearly every finish is food safe once cured. But projects that routinely have food in contact with them also are subjected to cleaning with soap and hot water, maybe a knife or other utensil, and generally experience more things that could destroy almost any finish than most pieces of furniture.

Cutting boards and charcuterie boards are going to have hard lives. Rather than use a finish that's impenetrable, I like to use a finish that's easy to renew. And for extra peace of mind, I like to use finishes on these projects that aren't harmful if ingested. Mineral oil makes a great finish for projects that come in contact with food, **Photo A**. The oil gives the wood a bit of luster and protection. And if the wood dries out from washing or general use, you can apply more with just a paper towel. You can buy mineral oil from the home center, but I've found the best prices in the pharmacy section (it's commonly sold as a laxative). You can also mix mineral oil and beeswax for a finish that feels a bit silkier. This mixture is often sold as butcher block finish. Stay away from other food-based oils, like olive oil, which can go rancid when exposed to the elements as a finish.

Applying these finishes is simple. First, raise the grain of the wood with water. Exposed to water and then dried, the wood's fibers will raise and

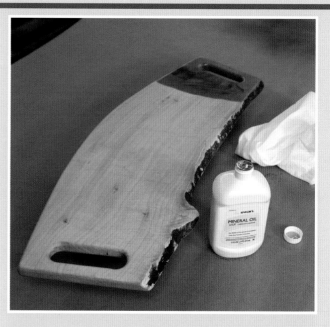

A. Plain mineral oil makes a fantastic food-safe finish. Though you can buy it at the home center, pharmacies also carry it.

feel rough. Sand the raised grain with a high-grit (220-grit or higher), then wipe a liberal amount of oil or oil/wax blend on the piece of wood, let it sit and soak in a bit. Some woodworkers put mineral oil in a tub and simply dip their projects for great saturation. Buff with a cotton cloth until the wood feels good and dry to the touch. Repeat the process when the board dries out after use and washing.

Furniture Finish

For a furniture finish, you're looking for something that enhances the grain of the wood and offers more protection. For a home woodworker, you also want to be cognizant of how the finish is applied and what the finish is made of.

A wiping varnish is a good finish for nearly all furniture projects, **Photo B**. This finish is available commercially under names like Danish oil or tung oil finish. It's made up of three main ingredients: an oil, a varnish, and a thinner. That also means you

B. Wiping varnishes are easy to apply and let you dial in the right amount of protection for any project.

can make your own (it's cheaper to do it this way if you're using a lot of it). The gist is that the three-part finish uses oil to enhance the wood grain, varnish to add a layer of protection, and a thinner to make the finish easy to wipe on.

Once you've sanded your project to 220-grit, pour a bit of finish on a cotton rag, and wipe it onto your piece. Wait a few minutes, then wipe it off with a clean cotton rag. Allow the finish to dry, then repeat. If you get dust nibs or the finish otherwise feels rough, just lightly sand in the direction of the grain with high-grit sandpaper (220-grit or higher), and apply more

C. Canned spray finishes let you quickly finish small projects, but larger projects benefit from a standalone spraying system if you have the space and budget.

finish. For a small table or shelves, three coats offer the best amount of protection. For a tabletop, you'll want more protection, so six or more coats offer the best protection.

One word of caution, though. As an oil-based finish cures it generates heat. So, when you're done with your rags, don't wad them up and throw them in the garbage (as it could start a fire). Instead lay the rags out flat on your driveway outside and allow them to dry completely before you throw them out.

Sprayed Finish

Spraying finish is the fastest way to finish a project. For smaller projects, I like to buy lacquer, shellac, polyurethane, or paint in a spray can, **Photo C**. Again, follow the directions on the can, but really, you just spray a few light coats (allowed to dry in between), and you're done.

For larger projects, I've invested in a finish sprayer and use water-based lacquer. If you have the space, it makes the finishing portion of a project go quickly. Look for a stand-alone HVLP spraying system (you can usually find them in the $300 – $500 range). The hardest part of using one of these is setting up an area for spraying and cleaning up the sprayer after you're done using it. During warmer months, I spray finish outside (making sure I'm far enough away from buildings and vehicles so I don't get overspray on them). When it's colder, I set up a corner of my heated shop with a window fan to create a negative pressure area, and spray projects there.

If you're just getting started, food-safe finishes, wiping varnishes, and canned spray finishes are the easiest to apply for these projects. If you have the budget and are making lots of projects, it might make sense to explore a finish-spraying system.

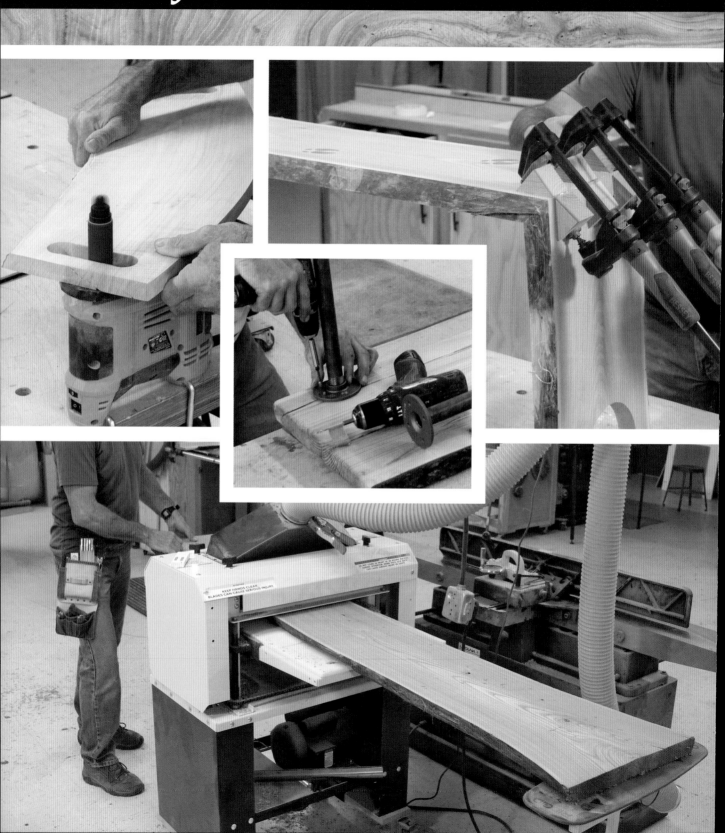

CHARCUTERIE BOARDS WITH EPOXY ACCENTS

SPECIFICATIONS

Dimensions	¾" x 10" x 28"
Material	Figured soft maple and epoxy
Finish	Odie's Oil

Tools used:

- Flexible curve
- Bandsaw or jig saw
- Drill press
- Forstner bit
- Jig saw
- Spindle sander
- Router
- ¼" roundover bit
- Heat gun

If you have smaller live edge pieces around — maybe something you milled yourself — a charcuterie board could be the perfect project for those slabs. Or, use a larger slab and get multiple boards out of it, as was done here. In addition to working with a live edge slab, this project covers shop-made hand holds in the board and epoxy accents.

Slab Choice

A charcuterie board is basically a fancy cutting board, except you don't cut on it. Your board could be as small as 9" x 13" or as large as you like. In addition to your design ideas, final size will be dictated by your slab selection. Since the board is being used for displaying food, not cutting food, you don't have to worry about the hardness of the wood. Any wood can make a good charcuterie board. As you decide on dimensions, keep in mind that many epoxies are not food safe. As a result, the area of your board you cover with epoxy shouldn't be used for displaying goodies. If you're planning on covering a lot of the board with epoxy, make it larger so you have enough real estate left for snacks.

A large slab, **Photo 1**, can be used to make a number of boards. You'll need a bandsaw or jigsaw to cut the slab, depending on its thickness. Cutting through the middle of the slab means each board will have only one live edge.

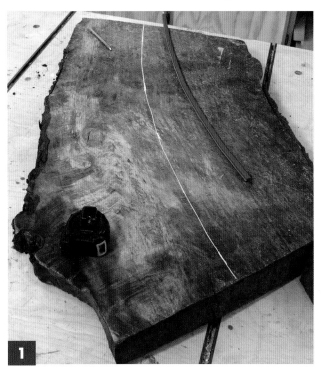

A large slab, like this piece of soft maple, will make multiple boards. Use a piece of chalk to sketch out how the boards will be cut from the slab.

Making the Boards

Get started on large, multi-board slabs by first cutting the slab into smaller parts, **Photo 2**. Thick slabs can then be resawn into thinner pieces using a bandsaw, **Photo 3**. After resawing (or if you're starting with thin stock) plane the boards to final thickness, **Photo 4**, and sand the saw marks off the cut edges, **Photo 5**.

The curve being cut on this piece mirrors the natural curves of the live edges. Leave the slab rough sawn for this step. Leveling the resulting smaller parts will be easier than leveling the large slab.

Resawing thick slabs into thinner pieces, instead of just planing them down, lets you get two boards from the slab.

Clean up and flatten the boards by running them through a planer.

Sand the edges as needed to remove saw marks.

Hand Holds and Edges

Make it easy to pick up and carry the board, and hang it on the wall to display it, by making hand holds. A comfortable size oval is 1¼" x 4½", ¾" from the edge of the oval to the edge of the board. Create the ovals using a Forstner bit, drill press, jigsaw, and sander.

Start the oval layout by locating the center of the oval relative to the end, **Photo 6**. Divide the width of the board in two and mark that centerline. Measure from that line to locate the center of the Forstner bit holes, **Photo 7**.

It's best to drill the holes on a drill press equipped with a fence, **Photo 8**. The fence guarantees uniform distance to the holes. After you've drilled the holes, use a straightedge to connect the edges of the holes, **Photo 9**, and a jigsaw to cut the hand holds out, **Photo 10**. Sand to remove the saw marks, **Photo 11**. Rout the corners with a ¼" roundover bit, **Photo 12**. Round over all the edges, including inside the hand holds, but not the live edge. Flip the board over and repeat the rounding process on the other face.

Mark the center of the oval 1⅜" from the end of the board.

Position the fence 1-⅜" from the center of the bit and drill both holes.

Locate the center of the Forstner bit holes by measuring and marking 1⅝" from the center line. Dimple the center point using a scratch awl.

Draw lines connecting the outer edges of both holes.

Use a jigsaw equipped with a fine-tooth blade and cut on the inside, the waste side, of the lines.

A spindle sander makes short work of sanding off the saw marks and finalizing the shape of the hand holds.

Rounding over the corners makes the board much more pleasant to hold and is also important for the epoxy work. The epoxy will waterfall over a rounded edge.

Epoxy Accents

Live edge charcuterie boards look great on their own, but an epoxy accent adds a nice flair and gives you a chance to let your creative juices flow. Calculate how much epoxy you need and choose your epoxy (Epoxy and Slabs page 32). It's better to have a little too much epoxy than not enough, so add another 20% or so and mix the required amount, **Photo 13**.

Pour the epoxy into small containers (small cups work great) and add color, **Photo 14**. Pour the

colors on your board and use your gloved finger to move the epoxy over the edges, **Photo 15**. You can also use your finger like a paint brush to mix the colors, **Photo 16**. Move a heat gun over the epoxy to remove bubbles and to move the epoxy, **Photo**

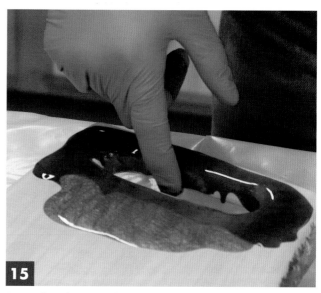

15

Epoxy doesn't want to flow over the edges, so you need to encourage it to do so. Move a light film of epoxy over the roundover and down the edges.

13

Follow the manufacturer's instructions and mix the two-part epoxy.

14

Use pigment and/or mica powder to add color to the epoxy. Pigment generally provides an opaque color, whereas mica powder creates a pearlescent look.

16

Move your finger through the colors to mix them and create patterns. Have fun!

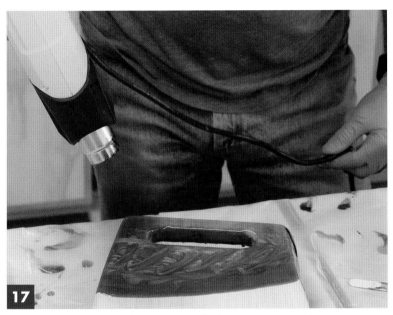

17

17, encouraging it to waterfall over the edges.

Finishing

Finish your charcuterie board with a food-safe oil, **Photo 18**. Products like mineral oil or walnut oil work well for these boards, as they're both food safe and are easy to renew if a board dries out. Don't use vegetable oil. Though food safe, it can go rancid if left exposed on the charcuterie board.

Use the air stream from a heat gun to push the epoxy over the edges, remove bubbles and level the epoxy surface.

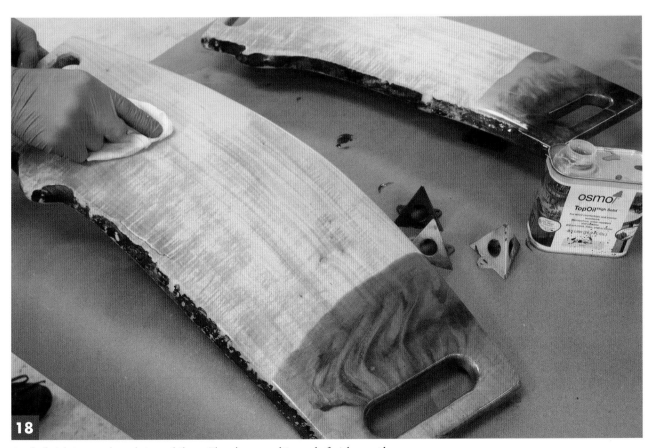

18

Apply finish to your boards to seal them. There's no need to apply finish over the epoxy.

MAGNETIC KNIFE BLOCK

SPECIFICATIONS

Dimensions	1" x 12" x 16"
Material	Cherry, spalted maple
Finish	Wipe-on polyurethane

Tools used:

- Rasp
- Tablesaw
- Miter saw
- Plunge router
- ⅝" guide bushing
- ⅜" router bit
- Biscuit joiner (countertop version)
- Keyhole router bit (wall hanging version)

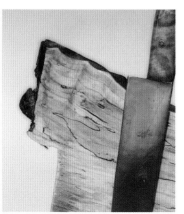

This project uses smaller live edge pieces and will be a great addition to any kitchen. It shows off your nice cutlery and people will be mystified by the knives magically sticking to the board. You can make the knife block so it sits on a countertop or gets used as a wall mount. Both approaches are shown.

Slab Choice

Grab your kitchen knives and the slab you plan on using. Make sure the slab will work for the project by laying your knives on it with a comfortable distance, 2" to 3", between each knife handle, **Photo 1**. The width of the board should be at least ½" more than the length of your longest knife.

As you choose the width of the slab keep in mind the typical spacing between countertops and upper cabinets, 18". The final height of the project will be the width of the slab plus the length of the knife handles. Make sure there's enough room in the spot you want the knife block before starting the project.

The Magnets

Part of the attraction of this project is that you can't see what's holding the knives in place. This is accomplished with rare earth magnets. Rare earth magnets are the strongest type of permanent magnet you can get. They come in many shapes and sizes, **Photo 2**. The magnets that work best for this project come in strips, 5 mm x 10 mm x 60 mm. You'll stick them together end to end, **Photo 3**, and double them up in thickness in the groove. Before starting the project check your knives to make sure they'll stick to magnets.

1

Check the viability of your slab for this project by laying your knives on it to make sure it's long enough and wide enough to work.

Prep the slab

You have many options for the slab you use for this project. The slabs shown here are 1" thick, but you could make a knife block with material as thin as ½" thick. You can leave the slab with two live edges if its width matches the length of your knives. For a wall hanging knife block the edges can be as wild as you like, but for the countertop knife block it's best if the lower edge is relatively straight. If all you have is a wide slab you can cut it narrower, leaving a live edge only on the top.

If you do cut the slab to width you can produce a faux live edge by making the cut with a bandsaw or jig saw. Don't worry about making the cut perfectly straight. In fact it'll look more natural if it's a bit wavy. Leave the saw marks on the edge. Use a rasp to knock down the front corner of the cut edge, **Photo 4**. Experiment on scrap before using this technique on your project to achieve the look you want.

Rare earth magnets are incredibly powerful and come in a variety of shapes and sizes.

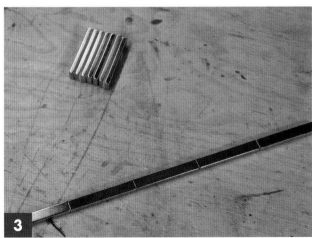

The magnets use for the knife block are formed into a strip, and will be doubled in thickness

Create a faux live edge by cutting the slab to width with a jig saw and using a rasp to rough up the corner of the slab.

Make a jig

The magnet groove is made using a shop-made jig and plunge router equipped with a guide bushing and ⅜" router bit, **Photo 5**. The jig, combined with the guide bushing, provides a lot of security for the cut. Once the guide bushing is engaged in the jig the router's travel is limited, so it's nearly impossible to mess up the cut.

Guide bushings are a very useful router accessory. They're commonly used in conjunction with dovetail jigs and work very well in any application where you want your router to follow a pattern. Guide bushings are available in a variety of diameters so you can match the bushing size to the task you're doing, with the guide bushing usually being ¼" larger than the bit you're using.

Make the jig from ½" material, MDF works great. Cut two sides 5" wide, 5" longer than your material. Make two spacers ⅝" x 3". This results in a groove that's 2" shorter than the slab. Dry assemble the jig components and make sure the guide bushing readily fits in the groove, **Photo 6**. Recut the spacers if necessary. Glue and clamp the jig when you have a good fit, **Photo 7**. Clean off the excess glue.

Rout the groove

Working on the back face of the slab locate and mark the top of the groove 1" from the top edge of the slab, **Photo 8**. Measure and mark the ends of the groove 1" from the ends of the slab, **Photo 9**. Make a ³⁄₃₂" spacer and position the jig, slab, and spacer so you can set the depth of cut, **Photo 10**.

With the router resting on top of the jig plunge until the bit touches the spacer and lock the stop rod, **Photo 11**. Cutting the groove within ³⁄₃₂" of the face is important. This gets the magnets close enough to the front face to work effectively.

5

The jig used to make the groove takes advantage of a plunge router, ⅝" guide bushing and ⅜" router bit.

6

Dry fit the jig components and make sure the guide bushing fits in the groove.

7

Glue and clamp the jig making sure the spacers remain flush with the adjacent surfaces.

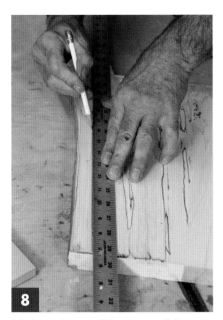

8 Mark out the top of the groove 1" down from the top edge of the slab.

9 Locate and mark the ends of groove.

10 Place the jig on the slab, and grab a 3/32" thick spacer block.

11 Set the depth of cut by plunging the router bit against the spacer and locking the depth stop rod on the turret.

Locate the jig on the slab by looking through its opening and positioning it on the groove lay out lines, **Photo 12**, so the groove will be cut below the line you made 1" from the top edge. Clamp the jig in place. Rout the groove in multiple passes, **Photo 13**, to make the magnet groove, **Photo 14**.

Glue in the magnets

The knife block will have the most effective grip on your knives if you completely fill the groove with magnets, end to end. If necessary, you can create shorter filler magnets by holding the strip in a vise, gripping it with pliers and snapping it, **Photo 15**. Rare earth magnets are brittle, and snap easily.

When you're ready to glue the magnets in get set up on a cast iron surface, like your tablesaw. Protect the surface from glue drips with a piece of scrap wood. Use two-part epoxy to glue the magnets into the groove, **Photo 16**. Eliminate the scrap piece and set the knife block directly on the cast iron, **Photo 17**. Allow the epoxy to cure.

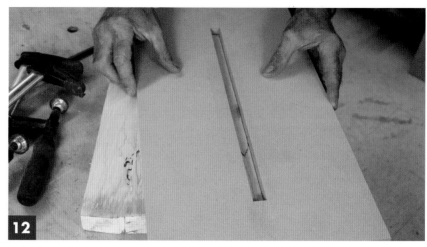

Sight through the opening in the jig to locate it on the layout lines on the slab. Clamp the jig in place.

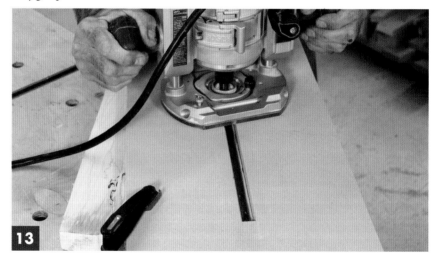

Rout the groove to its full depth in multiple passes, ⅛" to ¼" per pass.

The resulting groove is ready to receive the magnet strip.

Make the supports

The supports on the countertop version, ¾" x 4" x 10", are barely visible, so could be made from nearly anything. But if you have material left over from the knife block, use that and incorporate a live edge if you can, as shown here.

Stack the supports and cut them both at the same time, producing a 10-degree angle on the ends of the supports, **Photo 18**. Radius the top corner of the supports, **Photo 19**. Assorted sizes of flat washers make great radius gauges.

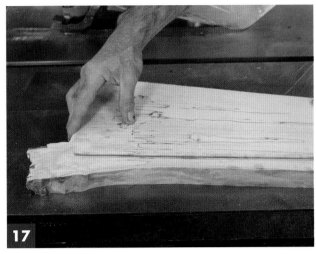

Place the knife block directly on a cast iron surface. This draws the magnets tight to the bottom of the groove.

Rare earth magnets are very brittle and snap easily. Clamp one in a vise and use pliers to snap and create shorter strips so you can completely fill the groove.

Cut a 10-degree angle on the bottom end of the supports.

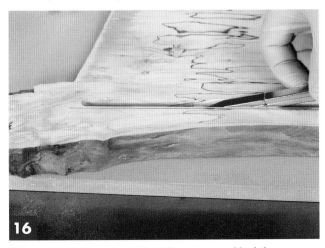

Mix two-part epoxy, spread it in the groove and bed the magnets in the epoxy. Note there are two layers of rare earth magnets.

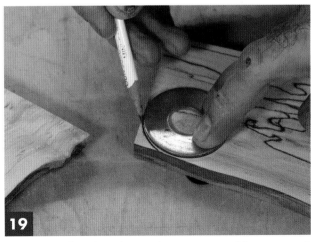

Mark, cut and sand a radius on the top corners of the supports. I trace a washer to get just the right radius.

Locate the supports 2" from the end of the slab. Use a biscuit joiner, **Photo 20**, and four #20 biscuits to join the supports to the back of the board. Glue the supports in place, **Photo 21**. Masking tape works great for "clamping" irregular surfaces like this.

Keyhole Slots

Keyhole slots can be used to fasten the wall-mount knife block to the wall. The slots are made using a keyhole router bit, **Photo 22**, plunge router and fence. With two keyhole slots on the back of the knife block you can slip the block over the heads of the mounting screws, and slide the knife block to the side to engage the screw heads in the slot. Practice making the slots on scrap before doing this on your project.

Make a line 2-½" from the top edge, with start and stop points marked 1" and 3" from each end, **Photo 23**. Install the keyhole bit in your plunge router and measure from the center of the bit to the edge of the base, **Photo 24**. This tells you how far the fence must be from the layout line. Use a piece of scrap wood as a fence (the groove jig works well) and clamp the fence to the slab in the correct location. Set the depth of cut to ⅜". Double-check that this is the correct depth for your keyhole bit, leaving ⅛" of material for the screw head to engage on.

Place the router base against the fence with the keyhole bit over the start position, **Photo 25**. Plunge the bit into the slab, move to the stop location, and allow the router to retract to pull the keyhole bit up through the work. You could use scrap wood as a fence to cut the magnet groove, but because of the multiple passes required to make this groove the jig is a preferred method.

Use the keyhole slot locations, **Photo 26**, to determine where the mounting screws should be positioned in the wall. Use appropriate screw anchors and mount your knife block.

Use a biscuit joiner to join the supports to the back of the knife block

Glue the supports to the knife block and use masking tape to clamp the supports to the board.

Use a keyhole router bit to create slots for hanging the wall mount knife block.

23

Lay out the locations of the keyhole slots.

24

Measure the distance from the center of the router bit to the edge of the router base.

25

Position the router base against the fence and plunge into the start point of the keyhole slot. Move to the stop point and allow the bit to exit the cut.

26

Measure the distance from the right hole on one slot to the right hole on the other slot to determine how far apart the screws in the wall should be.

DEER TRACK BENCH

SPECIFICATIONS

Height	18"
Length	48"
Width	11"
Material	Elm, 1½" thick, with walnut inlay
Finish	Shellac base coat, water-based lacquer topcoat

Tools used:

- Planer
- Framing square
- Track saw
- Biscuit joiner
- Beam compass/Trammel points
- Bandsaw or jig saw
- Spindle sander
- Slabstitcher inlay kit
- Router

Friends of mine recently bought a summer cabin, and I wanted to make them a cabin-warming gift. I knew they needed a mud room bench, and this project was born. Waterfall edges and deer track inlays make it truly unique.

Slab Choice and Prep

Look for a slab with characteristics that work with your project. The elm slab for this project, **Photo 1**, wasn't harvested from my friends' property, but elm does grow there. I love that connection. It's long enough to allow a waterfall on both ends, and the curved edge already looks like a bench seat. Elm is an under-utilized wood. It's relatively easy to work with, and the grain is beautiful. It's hard enough that it will hold up well as a bench or table.

Flatten the slab using a slab mill, or by sending it through your planer, **Photo 2**. If the slab has a bad twist or warp, start with a slab mill to remove the high spots before moving to the planer. If your planer isn't wide enough to accept the slab, do all the work with a slab mill. Take light passes as you get close to the final thickness. This provides the best surface finish and reduces sanding time.

This elm slab has great natural characteristics for this project. The curve is perfect for a bench seat, and the wide ends will make great feet.

Lay Out and Cut the Waterfall Edge

Do a rough layout of the legs and seat, **Photo 3**. Accurately mark the seat length but add 1" to the leg length to allow room for a final length cut later. At this point the project dimensions are still fluid. The final length of the legs should remain close to 18" to make the bench a comfortable height, but the length of the seat could change. If, when you do this layout, the waterfall miter falls directly on a knot or similar defect that could adversely affect the strength of the miter, change the length of the seat to avoid that.

Mark the final locations for the waterfall cuts, **Photo 4**. Since you can't square off a live edge, you'll need to use the center axis method. Mark out both ends of the seat. These lines also define the top end of each leg. Don't mark the final length of the legs yet. Use a sharp pencil to get an accurate line.

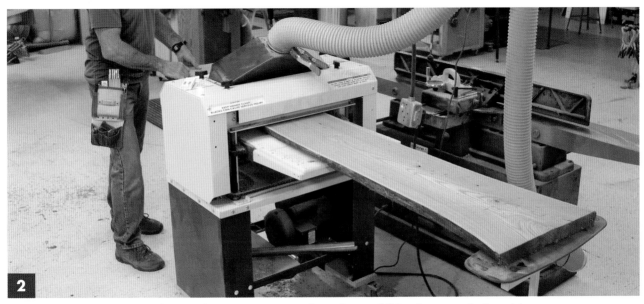

If the slab is relatively flat, like this one, clean it up using your planer. Set up additional supports for long slabs.

Use chalk to lay out the legs and seat on the slab. Chalk is very easy to see and wipes off easily if you change your mind. Use this preliminary layout to tweak your project dimensions as needed.

Mark out the locations of the waterfall edge cuts using one line for each joint.

Clamp the slab to your bench, support the outboard end, and cut the waterfall miter, **Photos 5 and 6**. Follow the procedures outlined in the Waterfall Edges chapter, being very careful to align your saw with the seat layout lines. Clamp the leg to your bench and cut the second miter. Measure and mark the final length of the legs. Set your saw to 90-degrees and cut the legs to length, **Photo 7**.

Clamp the slab to your bench and support the outboard end of the slab when cutting the waterfall miter. Don't let the offcut, the leg, fall to the floor.

Cut the leg miter. Carefully locate the track on the miter to minimize the amount of wood being removed. This optimizes the grain flow from the leg to the seat to produce the best waterfall.

Cut the legs to length. Be very careful to ensure the legs are identical.

Joinery and Shaping the Feet

Reinforce the waterfall miter with biscuits, **Photo 8**, centering the slots on the angled cuts of the miter. Be careful setting up your biscuit joiner and do test cuts in scrap. If the biscuit slot isn't correctly located, the slot can come through the face of the workpiece. That makes for a very bad day.

It's best to create distinct feet on furniture, rather than expecting a long, flat edge to meet the floor. If there are any irregularities in the floor your furniture will rock. To create the feet on this bench, find the center of the leg. Measure and mark 1" from the end grain, **Photo 9**, placing the 1" mark on the centerline of the leg.

This project has 2" wide feet. Set the compass to the width of the leg minus 4", center the compass on the layout lines and draw a circle, **Photo 10**. If the two legs aren't the same width do the compass calculation based on the narrower leg. Use the same size circle for both legs, allowing the width of the feet to vary slightly. As the scale of your project changes, change the size of the feet. A 24" wide slab for a coffee table should have 6" wide feet. Experiment with different size feet by drawing them on scrap or cardboard the same size as your slab to see how they look.

Cut the leg circles using a bandsaw or jig saw, and then sand off the saw marks, **Photo 11**. Cut on the waste side of the line, and sand to your pencil line.

Waterfall miters need to be reinforced. #20 biscuits are perfect for this project.

Draw a circle to create the feet. Notice that feet turn slightly in where they'll meet the floor, which adds a nice look to the feet.

Mark the circle center on the narrower of the two legs, 1" from end grain.

Cut the circles and sand off the saw marks.

Make Tracks

What could be more appropriate for a bench in a north woods cabin than deer track inlays? Working with the slab's natural characteristics, the curve in the deer tracks follows the curve in the live edge. Lay out the inlay pieces to get the look you want, **Photo 12**, and draw a square around each one.

Locate the template on your inlay layout lines and secure the template frame on the slab, **Photo 13**. Rout the recesses. Apply a light layer of glue in the recess, **Photo 14**, and tap the inlay pieces in. Excessive glue will create a big mess. Allow the glue to dry and sand the inlays flush.

12

When using multiple inlays place them all on your slab, changing their positions until you get the look you want.

13

Rout the inlay recesses into the slab. The deer track uses two templates, a left and right, to complete the inlay.

14

Put glue in the bottom of the recess and tap the inlay in. Very little glue is required for this.

Assembly, Sanding, and Finishing

Assemble the bench, **Photo 15**, by using the triangular scrap from the miter cut to create clamping cauls. Apply glue to the biscuits and miter joints and clamp. Remove the cauls once the glue is dry.

Sand the bench using a random orbit sander to do the bulk of the work. As a final sanding step knock the sharp corners off by hand sanding, **Photo 16**. This makes the bench a lot more comfortable to handle and sit on. Clean the sanding dust off the bench and apply the finish of your choice.

Create the cauls, then glue and clamp the waterfall edges. Tap the cauls to remove them after the glue is dry.

Knock down any sharp corners on the bench using 220-grit sandpaper on a sanding block.

SPECIFICATIONS	
Cookie dimensions	1½" x 26" x 40"
Material	Walnut
Bowtie	Copper
Leg height	14"
Finish	Brush on polyurethane

Tools used:

- Belt sander
- Slabstitcher copper inlay kit
- Router
- Wire wheel
- Mop sander
- Magnifying glass
- Cordless drill
- Beam compass/Trammel points

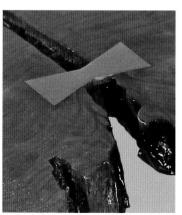

A log cookie makes a good-sized side table, with a great story to tell to boot. Log cookies are cross sections cut from a log. Cookies may also be referred to as rounds or log coins.

Growth rings are obvious in cookies, and they tell the tree's story. It's fun to count the growth rings and determine what was happening in history, or within your family, during the different phases of the tree's life. Log cookies also display heartwood and sapwood which, in many woods, are different colors and add visual interest to a project.

Log cookies typically crack while drying. The crack or cracks add an interesting element to the project and provide a spot for a bowtie or similar feature.

It's nearly impossible to dry log cookies without some cracks occurring, **Photo 1**. Here's a quick explanation of why this happens: The circumference of an annual ring is its tangential plane. The radius of an annual ring is its radial plane. As the cookie dries, shrinkage in the tangential plane is about 2X that in the radial plane. (This ratio varies across species.) The circumference of the cookie is shrinking faster than the radius, which introduces tension, which causes cracks. Since cracks are nearly impossible to avoid, embrace these defects and see them as interesting characteristics of your project. They can be filled with epoxy, bridged with bowties or even left alone if they're stable.

Leveling the Cookie

Log cookies are end grain, not face grain, so even if the cookie fits in your planer it shouldn't be planed. That wouldn't be safe (big chunks could get chipped out), and a planer would most likely tear the grain. It is OK to flatten a cookie with a drum sander or router-based jig. Any time you're sanding large pieces with a belt sander or random orbit sander, it's easy to spend too much time in one place and create high and low spots. Avoid this by drawing a series of heavy pencil lines on the piece before you start sanding, **Photo 2**. Keep the sander moving across the piece, staying in one spot only long enough to remove the pencil line, **Photo 3**. Draw a new pencil line after you've sanded off the original, and start over with the next grit.

Draw lines on the board before sanding to help you gauge how much material you've removed so you can keep the cookie flat.

Move across the piece, sanding off the pencil line as you go. Move to a new spot as soon as the pencil line has been removed.

Install a Bowtie

Cracks create the opportunity to add decorative details to the cookie. Bowties are a popular choice for this. Use bowtie templates to lay out a few options for the bowtie size and location, **Photo 4**. This is a great way to zero in on the look that you like best before making any cuts. Sand off the bowtie marks you won't be using, leaving behind the location you like, **Photo 5**.

Position the template over the lay out lines and make the cuts for the inlay, **Photo 6**. Be especially careful with the depth of cut for metal bowties so they end up flush with the surface of the cookie. They can be sanded flush, if need be, but it's best if they don't require a lot of sanding. If necessary clean up the routed recess with a chisel, and test fit the bowtie, **Photo 7**. Make additional adjustments to the recess as needed until you have a good fit. On metal bowties use 120-grit sandpaper to scuff the back face, **Photo 8**. This gives the metal some "tooth" to make sure it will bond with the glue.

Lay out test locations for the bowties to determine how many you want to use, where to place them and how large they should be.

Fasten the template to the cookie and cut the recess for the bowtie.

Remove extraneous marks once you settle on a bowtie size and location that you like.

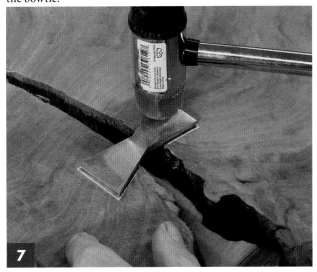

Test fit the inlay. Don't tap it in too far, or you won't be able to remove it.

8

Rough up the back face of metal inlays to make sure they have a good bond with the glue.

Standard wood glue can be used on wooden inlays or bowties. Two-part epoxy should be used on metal inlays, **Photo 9**. It's very important to read the instructions provided by the epoxy manufacturer regarding mixing and open time, how much time you have to work with the epoxy. Dab a little epoxy into the bottom of the bowtie recess, **Photo 10**. Don't use an excessive amount of epoxy. Insert the bowtie and gently tap it into the recess, **Photo 11**. If epoxy squeezes out, clean it up with denatured alcohol while it's still wet. It's very difficult to clean up epoxy squeeze-out after it has hardened. Sand the bowtie flush, **Photo 12**, if necessary. Be careful to not allow metal bowties to get hot while you're sanding them. It's possible to melt the epoxy and destroy the bond if the metal gets too warm.

9

Use two-part epoxy to glue in metal bowties. Follow the manufacturer's instructions for mixing.

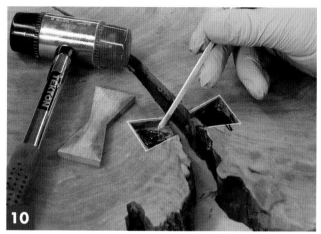

10

Put epoxy in the bowtie recess. It only needs to be applied to the bottom, not the sides.

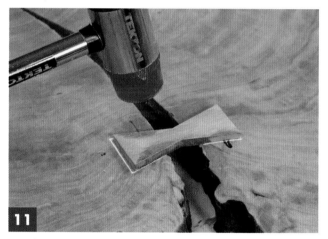

11

Tap the bowtie in place, seating it in the bed of epoxy. Use a soft-faced mallet, not a hammer.

12

Sand the bowtie as needed to make it flush, but don't allow metal bowties to overheat.

Edge Treatment

The live edge on this walnut cookie is exceptionally rough and textured. A wire wheel mounted in a cordless drill, **Photo 13**, provides a great way to clean up the texture. A wire wheel is more aggressive than a flutter sander, so it will reshape the live edge a little but still leave the edge plenty organic looking. Wire wheels are also a great way to knock any dirt, debris, or loose bark from the live edge. It's best to run a wire wheel in the same direction as the grain (up and down on a cookie, parallel to the face on a standard slab). Follow the wire wheel with a 240-grit flutter sander to smooth out any sharp points, **Photo 14**.

Count the Rings

Annual rings can be seen in any piece of wood, but they're especially evident in log cookies. It's fun to count the rings to see how old the tree was, **Photo 15**. It's easiest to count the rings after the cookie has been sanded smooth, but before finish is applied. The wood has a lot of contrast at that point, so it's easy to differentiate the individual rings. Growth rings can be very close together so a magnifying glass, **Photo 16**, is a huge help.

Counting the tree's rings tells you how old the tree was and allows you to place the tree's growth in important dates in history.

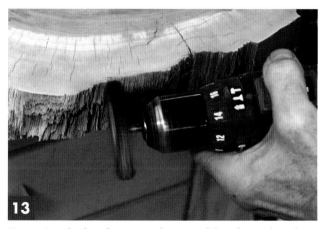

Use a wire wheel to clean up and remove debris from edges that are really rough.

Run a flutter sander over the edge to smooth out any sharp spots left by the wire wheel.

A magnifying glass helps you distinguish one ring from another, and a pencil helps keep track as you count.

Once you know the tree's age, create a timeline that points out important events in history, or in your family, **Photo 17**. Use a label maker to identify the events, and where in the tree's life they fell.

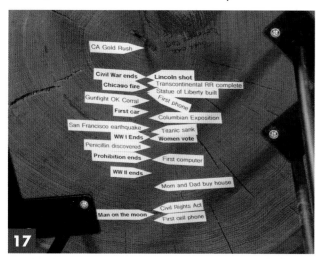

Add labels to identify significant points in history. The burr oak tree this cookie came from was a baby during the California Gold Rush.

Install Hairpin Legs

Apply finish to the cookie, and it's ready for legs. Hairpin legs, **Photo 18**, make turning slabs into tables very simple. They're commonly available as three rod or two rod legs. For short furniture like coffee tables (around 16" tall) two rod legs are fine. Three rod legs are better for tall tables, eliminating

flex in the leg so the table doesn't wobble. If black legs aren't what you want for your project, you can easily paint the legs with a metal-friendly aerosol paint in the color of your choice. Scuff sand the legs with 220-grit sandpaper before painting and wipe them down with denatured alcohol to remove any residue.

You can choose to use three or four legs on cookies that are round, or nearly round. This is an aesthetic decision. Many log cookie tables look better and less busy with only three legs. Another benefit of three-legged tables is that they can't wobble. When there are only three legs, they all touch the floor at the same time. This is also helpful if your cookie isn't perfectly flat.

Predrill and screw the legs onto the cookie, **Photo 19**. Use tape as a stop on the drill bit to make sure you don't drill through the slab. If the cookie isn't perfect round, locating the legs is subjective. Try them in a few different spots to see what looks best. On this walnut cookie it made sense to put the legs on the "high spots," the lobes projecting beyond the edge of the cookie. The fastening plate of the leg should be 2–4" from the edge of the cookie.

Hairpin legs provide a very easy way to turn a slab into a table. Three rod legs have less flex than two rod legs and should be used for tall tables.

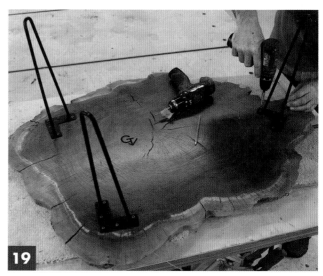

If the cookie isn't perfectly round position the legs based on the shape. This cookie has lobes projecting out slightly, providing perfect leg placement.

20

If the cookie is close to circular, lay out the leg locations using a beam compass, **Photo 20**. Locate the center of the cookie and set the beam compass to the radius of the circle you want the legs on. Don't change the beam compass from the radius measurement you used. Mark a starting point on the circle, a spot where you want a leg and, with the compass point on that spot, strike a short arc across the circle you drew.

Move the compass point to the new arc and strike another arc, moving around the circle to repeat the process. This divides the circumference of the circle into six even parts. Position the legs on the arc, **Photo 21**, using every other arc to get three evenly spaced legs, **Photo 22**. Attach the legs, and you have a side table that tells a story.

Position legs on a circular cookie using a beam compass and a little geometry. This approach evenly spaces three legs on a circle.

21

Use the arcs and the circle to position the legs.

22

This method provides three evenly spaced legs on your cookie.

DESK WITH PAINTED BASE

SPECIFICATIONS

Slab dimensions	1 ½" x 24" x 53"
Slab material	Curly hard maple
Base dimensions	22" x 51" x 28½" tall
Base material	Poplar
Slab finish	Shellac base coat, water-based lacquer topcoat
Base finish	Aerosol spray can black paint, semi-gloss

Tools used:

- Epoxy syringe
- Bar clamps
- Miter saw
- Table saw
- Router
- Tabletop fasteners
- Biscuit joiner

This design pairs a sturdy, traditional furniture base with a desk-sized slab. Part of the appeal of live edge slabs is how unique they are. With a unique looking slab, making a perfectly matching base can be a challenge.

Instead of trying to match the slab, go in another direction and make a base that contrasts the slab. This could be a painted base or, if you don't care for painting it, use a wood that looks completely different from the slab. This maple desk would have looked equally good with a walnut or cherry base. These dark woods completely contrast the curly maple slab.

Projects like this desk demand allowing for seasonal movement. The slab will be fastened to a base, but it can't be rigidly fastened. The slab has to be able to expand and contract with seasonal temperature and humidity changes, and we'll use special fasteners to allow for seasonal wood movement.

Slab Choice

A desk, or any kind of work surface, should be made from a hard wood. Common examples are maple, walnut, cherry, mesquite, and oak. There are many more choices. The slab used for this project is hard maple and has a lot going on, **Photo 1**. There are bark inclusions (the dark spots), lots of figure in the grain, and a very large crack.

The crack, **Photo 2**, certainly adds an interesting look, but could be impractical for a work surface. Bark inclusions, **Photo 3**, are just what they sound like, little bits of bark within the tree. Don't expect finish to fill these voids. It won't.

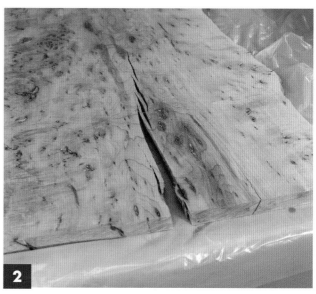

The decision to leave the crack as is, or fill it, is aesthetic. The slab will be fine with the crack left as is, but you wouldn't want to let pencils roll in that direction.

Hard maple is durable, and a great choice for a desk. There is lots of interesting character in this piece, from bark inclusions to a large crack.

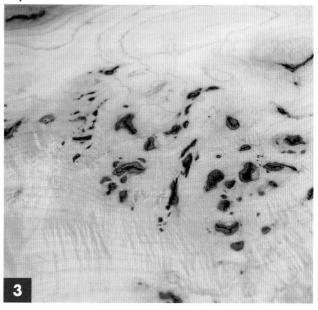

Bark inclusions add interesting visual detail, but each inclusion is a little valley that interrupts the flat work surface.

In this scenario — a slab full of fissures — use epoxy to get a perfectly flat work surface. Apply a tabletop epoxy with a syringe, **Photo 4**, to put a little epoxy into the valley of each bark inclusion. Dam the crack and use a deep pour epoxy to fill the crack, **Photo 5**.

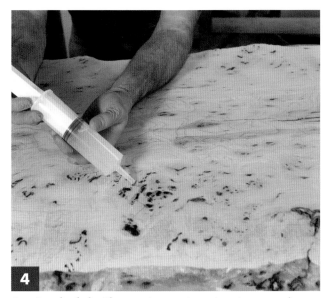

A syringe loaded with epoxy is a great way to get epoxy only where you want it…in each inclusion.

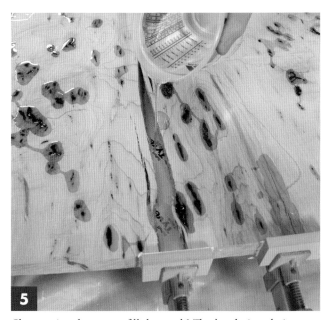

Clear or tinted epoxy to fill the crack? That's a design choice. This slab already has so much great character adding tinted epoxy may have been too much, so clear was chosen.

Build the Base

Build the base while you're waiting for the epoxy to cure. The slab isn't a perfect rectangle, and you need to keep that in mind as you're working on dimensions for the base. Take measurements in a few places, **Photo 6**, looking for the narrowest and shortest portions of the slab. Use those measurements to develop the size of the base. Allow for at least a 1" to 1½" overhang on each side.

Dimension the base using measurements from the narrowest and shortest part of the slab.

Poplar, **Photo 7**, is a great choice for paint-grade projects. Birch and maple are also good choices. The feature they have in common is that they're considered close grained woods. The pores won't absorb much paint, and this prevents the grain from raising and telegraphing through. With other woods (pine in particular) paint often causes the grain to telegraph through the paint, creating a textured surface. When building paint-grade projects, avoid open grain wood like pine and red oak.

Poplar machines well, is inexpensive and paints very well, making it a nice choice for painted projects.

Plane and joint the stock, and rip your legs and rails to width, **Photo 8**. The rails for this project are 4" wide. The legs are 1½" x 1½". Cut one end of each piece square, and cut the parts to final length, **Photo 9**. Rounding corners over with a hand-held router, **Photo 10**, is easy to do and makes the finished piece more user-friendly. It's much more pleasant to run your hand over rounded corners than sharp ones. From a design perspective a rounded corner is nice because it won't show wear (picture a vacuum bumping a leg) as quickly as a square corner.

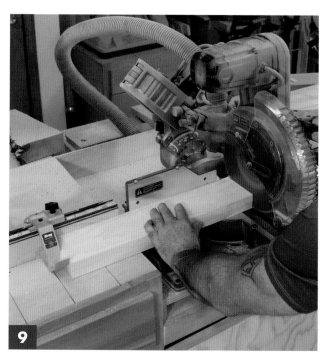

Use a stop block when cutting to final length to guarantee that parts with like dimensions come out the same.

Rip the legs and rails to width. ¾" thick stock is being used for the rails, and 1½" stock for the legs.

Rout a ⅛" roundover on the exposed corners of your project parts. Don't round the ends of the rails where they'll butt into the legs.

Allowing Seasonal Movement

One of the easiest ways to allow a solid wood slab to expand and contract with seasonal change is by using tabletop fasteners, **Photo 11**, to secure it to the base. The fasteners go in a groove in the cross rail, the rail that runs perpendicular to the grain of the slab. As the top expands and contracts across its width, the fasteners slide in the groove, allowing movement. Use your table saw to make the groove. Set the height of the blade to ⅜", position the fence using the fastener as a gauge, **Photo 12**, and make a test cut, **Photo 13**. Check your setup, **Photo 14**. Adjust the rip fence as needed, make additional test cuts and, when the setup is correct, cut grooves in your project pieces, **Photo 15**.

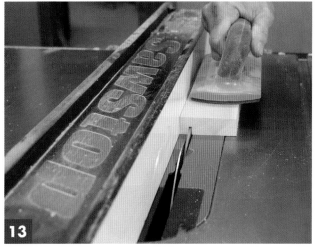

Do a test cut in scrap.

Tabletop fasteners, also call Z clips, allow the desktop to expand and contract independently of the base.

When the groove is in the correct spot there will be a small gap below the bottom flange of the fastener as you hold it tight to a horizontal surface.

With one flange of the fastener held against the rip fence, position the fence so the other flange is not quite to the saw blade.

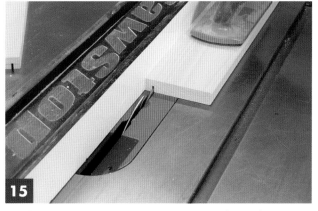

Cut the groove in your project pieces once you know the setup is correct.

Joinery

There are many options for joining the legs and rails on this desk, including mortise and tenon, pocket holes, and biscuits. A biscuit joint was chosen, with one #20 biscuit in each joint.

Having a reveal (a small step) between the faces of the rails and the faces of the legs is a nice design touch. This is easy to do with a biscuit joiner.

Using scrap that's the same thickness as your rails rest the biscuit joiner fence on a piece of ¼" plexiglass and center the cutter on the material, **Photo 16**. Make a test cut and adjust the fence position if necessary. Cut the biscuit slots in your rails with the plexiglass in place, **Photo 17**. Any ¼" material will provide the required spacing, but it's convenient to do this trick with plexiglass because the layout lines can be seen through it.

Leave the fence in the same position it was in for the rails and, without using the plexiglass, cut biscuit slots in the legs, **Photo 18**. This automatically provides a ¼" reveal, **Photo 19**. You can change the size of the reveal by changing the thickness of the spacer used.

Sand the pieces, making sure you've removed all machining marks and pencil lines. Sand the base to 180-grit to prepare for paint.

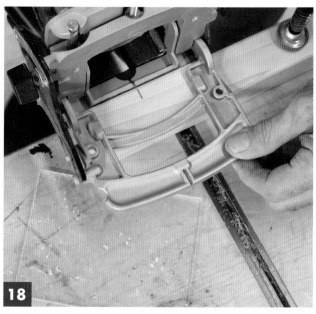

18

Set the plexiglass aside and cut biscuit slot in the legs.

16

Set up the biscuit joiner for the rail cuts with a piece of plexiglass between the fence and the material.

17

Cut biscuit slots in the ends of all your rails with the plexiglass between the fence and the workpiece.

19

Using the plexiglass spacer automatically provides a reveal equal to the thickness of the spacer.

Assembly

This project has a lot of pieces, so it's best to assemble it in stages, **Photo 20**. Rosin paper protects your bench from squeeze out. Use a mallet to tap the rails into alignment on the legs and use clamp pads to prevent the clamps from marking the wood. Tighten the clamps a small amount and check the leg/rail assembly for square. Adjust as needed before snugging the clamps. Look closely for glue squeeze out. If you have squeeze out allow it to dry a little, to a rubbery consistency, and slice it off with a putty knife. Do the final assembly with the base upside down on a bench, **Photo 21**, again using clamp pads and checking for square. After the glue is dry remove the clamps and do final sanding as needed.

Assemble the two end sections of the base first, checking them for square as you snug the clamps.

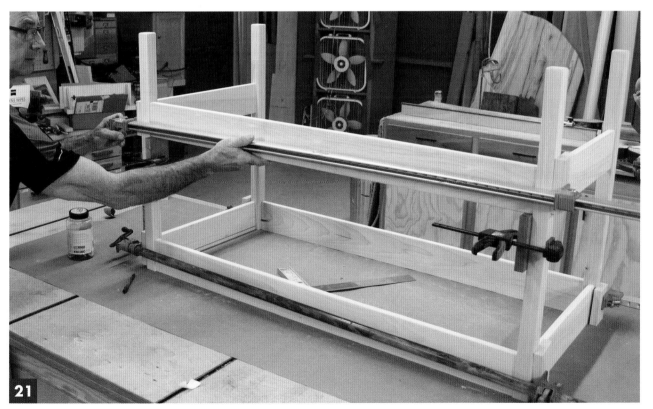

Get extra "hands" for the final assembly by clamping blocks to the legs for the rail to rest on. Be sure to remove these blocks as soon as the rail is clamped so they don't end up accidentally glued to the legs by squeeze out.

Painting

Place the base upside down on a bench covered with rosin paper and partially drive one wood screw into the bottom of each leg, leaving 1" of screw sticking out. Paint the bottom surfaces of the legs and rails, **Photo 22**. Standard cans of aerosol paint work great for projects like this and provide better results than brushing or rolling the paint. Make sure the paint is compatible with wood. A trigger for the aerosol can, available where most paint is sold, is worth its weight in gold when doing this much spraying.

Stand the base upright and finish painting, **Photo 23**. This is the benefit of the woodscrews in the legs—the desk can be flipped upright while the paint is still wet, and the legs won't stick to the rosin paper. You'll probably need to do multiple coats to completely cover the wood. The first coat may feel a little rough. If it does, sand the base lightly with 220-grit paper before applying additional coats.

Begin painting with the base upside down. Get paint on all surfaces you won't have access to when the base is upright.

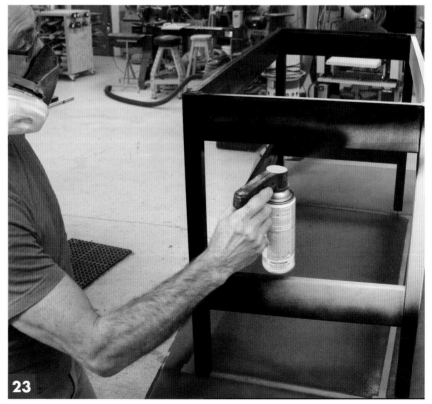

Flip the base over and paint the remaining surfaces.

Final Sanding and Assembly

When the epoxy is fully cured (make sure to read the directions included with your epoxy), sand the excess off the surface. Start with a belt sander, **Photo 24**, and finish with a random orbit sander, **Photo 25**. Use a sanding block with 220-grit sandpaper to take the knife edge off of the live edge, **Photo 26**. Apply your finish to the slab, on both the wood and the epoxy.

Place the slab with its good face down on your bench. Be sure to protect the slab with carpet scraps, or similar, between the bench and the top. Center the base on the bottom of the slab, **Photo 27**. Predrill for the tabletop fastener screws, and install the fasteners, **Photo 28**. Don't overtighten the screws. If you make them too tight the flange of the fastener can embed in the rail and limit the movement of the top. Stand it upright and enjoy your desk!

26

The angle of a live edge can leave a really sharp corner. Remove the corner with hand sanding.

27

Center the base on the slab. This can be a little tricky on slabs with irregular edges and sometimes requires a bit of a judgement call.

24

A belt sander will make short work of removing excess epoxy from the surface.

25

Wrap up the sanding with a random orbit sander. Most epoxy manufacturers recommend sanding to 220-grit, no finer, or finish won't stick to the epoxy.

28

Put masking tape on the bit being used to predrill for screws to prevent drilling through the top. Drive the screws holding the fasteners in place. They should be snug, but not overtightened.

STEEL PIPE SHELF

SPECIFICATIONS

Height	68"
Width	28"
Depth	16"
Shelf thickness	1½"
Material	Douglas Fir, ¾" black pipe
Finish	Watco Danish Oil

Tools used:

- Electric chainsaw (if desired)
- Planer
- Router table
- MatchFit clamps
- Table saw
- Large speed square or framing square
- Cordless drill
- Large pliers or pipe wrench

A narrow slab, cut into sections, makes great stock for a shelving unit. Combine live edge pieces with readily available steel pipe to get a functional piece of furniture with an industrial twist.

Making a set of shelves requires a slab that's long and relatively narrow, **Photo 1**, or a slab that's wide enough for you to cut the shelves from it, providing the width you need. Shelving units that will be used for books are typically at least 12" deep, but the depth of shelves can vary from 6" to 24", depending on how you'll use them. Working with a single, long slab gives you the option of leaving the live edge on both edges, something you may want to do if the unit will be freestanding, not against a wall. Base the length of the shelves on what you'll be storing on them or the space the finished unit has to fit into.

Prep the Parts

Instead of cutting the shelves to length with a circular saw, consider cutting them with a chainsaw, **Photo 2**. The chainsaw gives the end grain a rough-hewn look, **Photo 3**, that is a nice fit with the industrial look of the completed shelves. Notice the prevalent cracks in these pieces. There's nothing wrong with simply leaving the cracks as they are, but in this case the cracks are so large they may weaken the slab to a point where it falls apart. Creating dams and pouring tinted epoxy into the cracks, **Photo 4**, solves the problem. After the epoxy has cured, sand off the high spots and plane the material to your desired shelf thickness, **Photo 5**. The thicker you leave the shelves, the longer they can span. ¾" thick material can span up to 30" and take a reasonable load without sagging. As a rule of thumb, shelf spacing generally ranges from 7" to 15", with 8" to 12" being common for book shelves.

Look for long and relatively narrow pieces for a shelf project.

Crosscut the slab with a chainsaw to give the shelf ends an extremely rough sawn look.

The chainsaw leaves the ends very rough. This will be scuff sanded later to knock off sharp points.

Pour epoxy into large cracks to stabilize the wood. Tinted epoxy creates an interesting contrast against the material.

Make a straight-line edge jig

Ripping irregular edged pieces can't be done on a tablesaw, unless you have a straight-line jig for the saw. This jig is easy to make and incorporates Matchfit Dovetail Clamps, made by MicroJig. The clamps seat in dovetail-shaped slots and allow you to secure odd-shaped pieces so you can safely cut them.

Cut a piece for the base of the jig. MDF works well, and a piece ¾" x 20" x 32" is a practical size. You can go larger or smaller depending on your needs. MicroJig provides good instructions for creating jigs and working with their clamps. Use a router table to cut dovetail slots 3" from each edge, **Photo 6**. The jig, **Photo 7**, helps with this project, and will be a useful addition to your shop.

You could, alternatively, rip the shelves to width using a circular saw or track saw.

Rout dovetail slots in the base of the straight-line jig

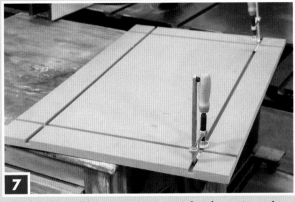

This simple jig allows you to put a straight edge on irregular edge pieces.

Plane the shelves to final thickness.

Straight-Line the Shelves

Place your material on the jig and measure from the edge of the jig to the bark, **Photo 8**, to position it. Do this on both ends to make the cut edge parallel to the bark edge. Another benefit of this jig is that you can clamp parts at an angle if you want to produce a taper. Tighten the clamps and make the cut, **Photo 9**. You can vary the width on the shelves, graduating the size from a wide shelf on the bottom to a narrower shelf on top, or keep them all the same. If you do graduate the width of the shelves, it works best to change the width of each shelf by a consistent amount. For instance, make each shelf 1" narrower than the shelf below it. The same idea can be applied to the length of the shelves with the longest shelf on the bottom, and shortest on top.

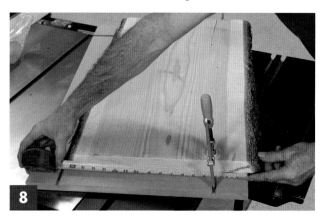

Position the slab on the jig, measuring from the edge of the jig to the bark. Clamp it in place.

Cut your shelves. You can make them the same width, or graduate the widths.

Sand and Pre-Drill

The chainsaw cut creates a cool rough sawn end, but maybe a little too rough sawn. Knock down the splinters, but leave the ends looking rough-hewn, by sanding the ends with 60-grit sandpaper, **Photo 10**. If you're happy with the look and feel of the chainsaw cut, there's no need to sand. It's purely an artistic choice.

It's easiest to assemble the shelf unit if you've already pre-drilled for the pipe flanges (instead of trying to locate them as you go). In addition to making assembly easier, using a jig for the flange layout will keep the pipes vertically aligned, like columns, top to bottom. The jig also helps with non-square boards, as the chainsaw-cut ends and live edge can make measuring for each flange location a challenge. If you graduate the shelf width or length this isn't as critical, because the pipes probably won't be in line with each other. Graduated shelves may require a template for some of the flange locations, but not all of them.

Sand the ends with 60-grit sandpaper. This aggressive grit will smooth them slightly, but still leave a rough look.

Cut a piece of plywood that's large enough to encompass the flange locations, lay it on your stack of shelves and experiment with flange positions, **Photo 11**. The edge of the flange should be at least ¼" away from the ends and edges of your shelves, but there's no set rule for the set back of the flanges. When you're happy with the layout, use a square to mark the center line of the flanges on the template, **Photo 12**, and mark the two screw hole locations that fall on the line. The straight cut made on one edge of each slab simplifies doing this layout. Take your measurements from that edge. When the layout on the template is complete, transfer the flange center lines to the edges of the shelves, **Photo 13**. Align the center lines on the template with the lines on the shelf edge and drill through the template at each screw location, **Photo 14**. Use tape on the drill bit to set the depth of the hole. Remember that the top shelf gets holes drilled only on its bottom face.

Mark the flange centers and screw hole locations with the flange centers equidistant from the ends of the shelves.

Center the template on the length of the shelves and transfer the flange center lines on the template to the edges of the shelves.

Use a piece of plywood to create a template for the flange locations.

Pre-drill each shelf for the flange screws.

Working with Pipe

Steel pipe offers lots of design opportunities. Home centers carry an array of diameters, usually ¼" to 2", and a variety of lengths, **Photo 15**. Fittings such as 45-degree and 90-degree elbows, floor flanges (used on this project) and couplers are available. The diameter refers to the inside diameter of the pipe. Change the look and contrast by choosing galvanized or black pipe. Galvanized pipe is slightly more expensive. Visit the plumbing department at a home center to get a feel for what's available before starting your project. ¾" pipe in 12" and 18" lengths was used for this project, with two floor flanges on each pipe.

Steel pipe can be greasy and dirty. Clean the parts with naphtha or a similar solvent before working with them. Build the pipe columns for the shelf by threading a floor flange onto each end of the pipes, **Photo 16**. Grip one flange in a vise and use a wrench on the other flange to snug the system. It doesn't need to be made overly tight, just enough to eliminate any wiggle between the components. Be careful to not mar the flange with the wrench. Stand the assemblies up on a workbench and check that they're close to being the same length, **Photo 17**, so the spacing provided by the pipes remains consistent and you don't get a wobble in the shelf.

Clean the pipes and flanges, and thread a flange onto each end of the pipe.

Steel pipe is available from home centers in different diameters and lengths, and as galvanized (left) or black pipe.

Check the lengths of the pipe/flange assemblies to make sure they're all the same. Adjust as needed.

18

Screw the pipe columns to the bottom of each shelf.

First, sand and finish the shelves. This is much easier to do before you put the shelves together. Next, assemble the shelf unit by screwing the flanges to the bottom of the shelves, **Photo 18**, using the holes you drilled with the template. Protect the shelves with carpet scraps on your workbench. Pre-drill for the other two holes in each flange and drive those screws. Flat head drywall screws, 1" long, work well for black pipe. Use galvanized screws on galvanized pipe. After the pipe column is fastened to the shelf check the flanges on the opposite end of the pipe.

Use the wrench to rotate the flange until the holes align front to back, **Photo 19**. This puts the holes in the same orientation as the holes that were pre-drilled earlier using the template. It may create a tiny change in the overall length of each assembly, but not enough to adversely affect the shelf unit. Assemble the shelf unit from the bottom up. Put the shelf and its pipe columns in place, locate the flanges over the existing screw holes and drive the screws, **Photo 20**. Pre-drill and drive the remaining screws.

If the shelf unit rocks, adjust the pipe/flange assemblies that extend from the bottom shelf to the floor to eliminate the wobble.

19

Align the holes in the flanges so they'll line up with the hole locations you made with the template.

20

Position the flanges over the template screw holes and fasten the flange in place.

FLOATING SHELVES

SPECIFICATIONS

Dimensions	1 ½" x 9" x 28"
Material	Hackberry
Hardware	Floating shelf hardware
Finish	Lacquer

Tools used:

- Table saw
- Draw knife
- Dado head
- Self-centering dowel jig
- Cordless drill
- Brad point drill bit
- Clamps
- Level
- Wall anchors

A floating, live-edge shelf adds a refined, yet rustic look to any room. With no visible support, floating shelves have an almost magical look.

Since no hardware can be seen, there's nothing to detract from the beauty of the wood you choose. If you have a slab with a few bad spots, **Photo 1**, this a good spot to use it. You can cut around the defects to produce the smaller pieces required for floating shelves.

A wide variety of floating shelf hardware is available online and from woodworking specialty stores. Make sure your hardware, **Photo 2**, is on hand before starting your project. The functionality of the hardware is very similar regardless of what brand you buy. It consists of a bracket with one or more rods fastened to it. The bracket gets fastened

to the wall, and the rods project into the shelf to support it. The allowable thickness and width of the shelf varies from manufacturer to manufacturer, along with how much weight the bracket is capable of supporting. Longer shelves require longer wall hardware. The back edge of the shelf is machined to accept the rods and to hide the wall bracket. Follow the specific instructions for your kit. Here are tips to help you along.

Prep the Shelves

Cut the shelves to length and use the straight-line edge jig (page 119) to rip them to width, **Photo 3**. Make sure the depth of the shelf is compatible with the hardware you purchased. Plane the shelves to thickness, again paying attention to the parameters provided with your hardware kit. A maximum thickness is sometimes given, and a minimum is always given. The shelf must be thick enough to hide the hardware. Plane a piece of scrap while you're planing the shelves and make it the same thickness as the shelves. It'll be used later for test cuts. If the bark on the live edge is loose use a draw knife to remove it, **Photo 4**.

This slab has a few bad spots, making it a great candidate for the smaller components required for floating shelves.

Purchase the floating shelf hardware before starting your project.

Rip the shelves to width using the straight-line edge jig.

Machine the Shelf for the Bracket

The floating shelf hardware can be concealed in a groove in the back of the shelf. The groove can be cut using a dado head in a tablesaw or a router bit in a router table. Use a dado head or router bit that is slightly larger than half the width of the bracket. If the bracket is 1" wide use a ⅝" cutter.

Set the depth of cut to slightly more than the thickness of the wall bracket, **Photo 5**. It's easier to feel this than to measure it. Position the wall bracket next to the dado head or router bit and raise the cutter until you can feel that it's slightly (about ¹⁄₃₂") higher than the bracket.

Measure the width of the bracket, subtract that from the thickness of the shelves, and divide the result by two to get the distance you need from the fence to the cutter. For instance, a 1" wide bracket being used with a 1½" thick shelf requires ¼" between the fence and the cutter. Set the fence at this location and position a feather board to help keep the material tight against the fence. Make two cuts in the scrap piece, **Photos 6 and 7**, rotating the piece end for end between cuts so the opposite face is against the fence for the second cut.

Check the bark on the live edge and peel it off it it's loose.

Install a dado head in your table saw and set its height to slightly more than the thickness of the back bracket.

Position the rip fence and make a cut in the test piece.

Rotate the test piece end for end and make a second cut to complete the groove.

The bracket should easily drop into the groove and the walls of the groove should be slightly above the bracket, **Photo 8**. Make necessary adjustments and do additional test cuts as needed before cutting the shelves. When the setup is correct, cut the grooves in your shelves, **Photo 9**.

8

Check the fit of the bracket.

9

Cut the grooves in the shelves.

Drill for the Rods

Locate the bracket on the shelf by measuring the rod-to-rod distance, subtracting that from the overall shelf length and dividing the result by two, **Photo 10**. This provides the distance from the end of the shelf to the center of the first rod. For example, if the rod-to-rod distance is 18", and the shelf is 28" long, the center of the rod is located 5" from the end. Make a mark that distance in from the end and position the rod on that layout line, **Photo 11**. Keep the hardware in that position and transfer the location of the second rod to the shelf, **Photo 12**. It's easier and more accurate to transfer the location than to measure and mark. The hardware relies on holes for the rods being accurately located and drilled in the back of the shelf. Missing the location of these holes could make the shelf useless, so be very careful with this step.

10

Measure the rod to rod distance.

11

Position the hardware on the shelf by aligning the rod with the layout line that centers the hardware on the shelf.

12

Mark the location of the second rod on the shelf.

Check the hardware to see what size hole must be drilled. A self-centering dowel jig works great for making the holes perpendicular to the edge of shelf. Align the jig with the rod layout lines and drill a hole with the correct size drill bit, **Photo 13**. The rods are typically so long that you won't be able to drill to the depth the rod requires with the jig clamped on the shelf. Remove the jig and, allowing the drill bit to follow the first hole, continue drilling, **Photo 14**, until the hole is deep enough for the rod. Repeat this process for the second rod. You'll be able to drill to full depth without removing the dowel jig if you drill the holes with an extra-long (12") drill bit, **Photo 15**. These are available online and at woodworking specialty stores.

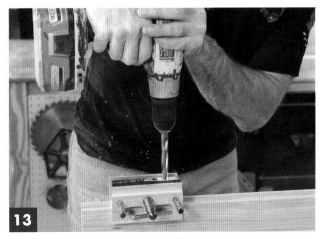

13

Position the correct size hole in a self-centering dowel jig over the rod location lines and drill a hole.

14

Remove the dowel jig and continue drilling to the depth required for the rod.

15

You can avoid the two-step drilling process by using an extra-long brad point bit.

Make sure the hardware works in the holes, **Photo 16**. If it doesn't slide in easily you may be able to slightly enlarge the holes with the drill bit so they'll accept the rods, but this isn't a good practice and can cost you stability of the shelf.

Double-check the fit of the hardware in the shelf.

Plug the Groove

The groove that receives the bracket was cut all the way through the shelf, end to end, and will show on the end of the shelf when it's mounted on the wall. It can easily be plugged so the groove is hidden. Plane an offcut from the shelves until it snugly fits into the groove, **Photo 17**. Cut strips from the planed piece so the thickness of the strip matches the depth of the

Make a plug for the groove by planing an offcut from the shelves until it just fits in the groove.

groove. Cut a short piece from the strip and glue it in the groove, **Photo 18**. Make sure the plug is short enough to prevent it from interfering with installing the hardware. It's a good idea to cut a number of strips so you have options and can match color and grain to help make the plug less obvious, **Photo 19**.

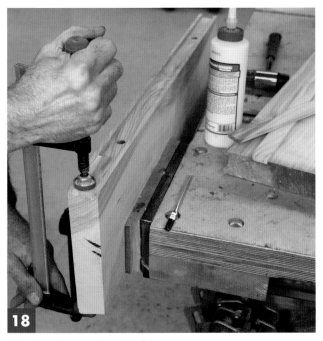

Glue the plug into the end of the groove.

Make careful selections on the plug material and they'll be nearly invisible on the ends of the shelves.

Install the Shelves

Check the manufacturer's instructions for specific details on installing the hardware. Choose fasteners based on the wall the shelves are being placed on. When possible, screw the hardware into a wall stud, but drywall or concrete anchors also work fine.

Use a level and mark lines on the wall to locate the hardware. Position the hardware on the line and trace the screw hole locations, **Photo 20**. Different anchor systems require different kinds of pre-drilling. Match the drill to the fastener and pre-drill at each screw location, **Photo 21**. Mount the hardware to the wall, **Photo 22**, and slide the shelves onto the hardware posts, **Photo 23**.

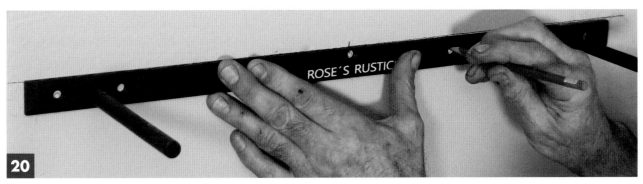

Align the hardware with level lines you've put on the wall and mark the hole locations.

Pre-drill for the fasteners.

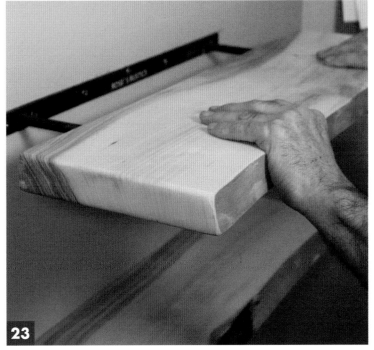

Install the shelves.

Drive the fasteners to secure the hardware to the wall.

BOOKMATCHED DINING TABLE

SPECIFICATIONS

Height	30"
Length	64"
Width	32"
Thickness	1"
Material	Black walnut, cast aluminum legs
Finish	Osmo Top Oil

Tools used:

- Long level or straightedge
- Track saw
- Biscuit joiner
- Bar clamps
- Portable drill guide
- Ratchet
- Cordless drill with sanding disc

Industrial-style metal legs are the perfect match for a live-edge slab. These reproduction legs, made from aluminum, are lighter (and less expensive) than true antiques.

When you have access to sequentially cut slabs (pieces that were adjacent to each other in the tree), you can create a bookmatched project. Like the pages of an open book, bookmatching provides two or more pieces with mirror image grain, **Photo 1**. As you're working with the slabs you need to find the faces that match. Of the four available faces on two slabs, two will provide a mirror image, two will not. Look for distinct characteristics like knots, sapwood or grain patterns to determine which faces match.

The two slabs will be joined along a straight edge to create a tabletop. Once you know which faces match you have two choices for joining the slabs to maintain the bookmatch. Position the boards so you can see the bookmatch and allow the edges to overlap, **Photos 2 and 3**. Both of these options provide a bookmatch but result in different looking tables. In addition to changing which edges to overlap you can vary the amount of the overlap. This process is done to show where you'll need to cut the slabs to create the glue joint. Take your time experimenting with the layout to make sure you get what you want.

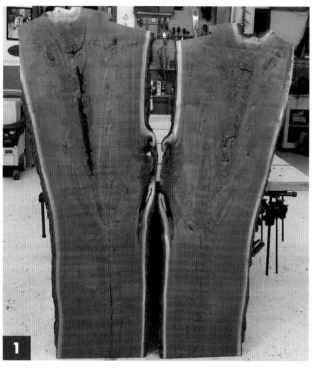

Sequence cut slabs provide bookmatched pieces, meaning the grain in each piece is a mirror image of the other piece.

Determine which edges you'll join by overlapping the slabs. This option provides a more rectangular table and keeps the curly edge grain present in the live edge.

Overlap the other two edges to check your second option. This approach will remove the curly grain and create a more bell-shaped table.

Lay Out and Cut the Slabs

When you lay out the cut lines on the slabs it's important to remove the same amount of material from each slab in order to maintain a mirror image that's centered on the final tabletop. Measure carefully, and then mark out the cut lines, **Photo 4**. This step, and the amount of material you remove, also determines the final width of the tabletop.

4

Lay out the location of the cut lines on the slabs.

When working with large slabs you won't be able to clean up sawn edges using a jointer, so it's important to get good cut quality right off the saw. The best solution for this is to make the cuts using a track saw, **Photo 5**. If the slabs are small enough that the edges can be jointed on a jointer, the quality of the rip cut isn't as critical.

5

Make the cuts using a track saw. Be sure the blade is sharp, so you have good cut quality for the glue joint.

There are also different options regarding the length of the slabs. Two sequence cut slabs should already be the same length and may still have the original chainsaw cuts on each end. If you plan on keeping the existing ends as part of your final project, no length cut is needed. If the slabs are significantly longer than what you want as a final size, rough cut them about 2" longer than the final dimension. The slabs being used here each have a chainsaw cut on one end and have been cut to rough length with a circular saw on the other end.

Epoxy Where Needed

These walnut slabs have a lot of character, including a very large bark inclusion and a bunch of cracks. If cracks, holes, or recesses in the tabletop don't bother you, you can leave them alone. Alternatively, you can use epoxy to create a seamless and flat top. The bark inside the inclusion has a very interesting texture, and it would be a shame to completely cover it. To preserve the visual depth of the inclusion, use clear epoxy, **Photo 6**. The cracks in the walnut slabs appear as dark lines in the wood. Use black tinted

6

Pour clear epoxy into recesses that you want to be able to see into after the epoxy is cured.

epoxy here so the cracks blend with the surrounding wood, **Photo 7**. Like most epoxy work, this is an aesthetic decision. You could just as easily pour epoxy mixed with any color pigment you choose, or with mica powder.

Allow the epoxy to cure and sand off the excess, **Photo 8**. A belt sander makes short work of this, but a random orbit sander would also work. Start with 80-grit paper and work through the grits up to 220-grit.

Pour colored epoxy to create an accent, or to blend the epoxy with the natural colors of the wood.

Use a belt sander to remove excess epoxy from the surface.

Joinery and Glue Up

There's no need to add reinforcement to a good glue joint. Today's glues are stronger than the wood you're joining. But adding biscuits to the joint, **Photo 9**, will help keep the surfaces aligned as you're doing the glue up. This is especially important on a large glue up like this tabletop. If the surfaces end up uneven at the glue joint you'll have lots of sanding to do later to level them. Position the biscuits every 6" – 8" along the joint.

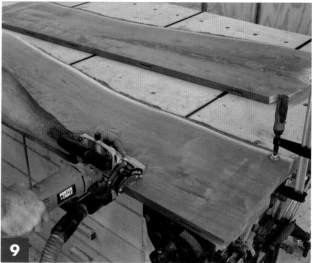

Adding biscuits to the joint will help the glue up go much easier. They provide registration, keeping the faces of the boards aligned.

Do a test assembly to check your work, then apply glue and assemble the tabletop, **Photo 10**. Wooden clamp pads would probably mar and compress the slabs' live edges. Instead use 2" rigid foam, available at home centers, for clamp pads. It's firm enough to allow the clamps to squeeze the joint closed but acts as a cushion, preventing the live edges from being distorted. Add a small clamp at each end of the glue up, using it to bridge the seam, **Photo 11**. This helps keep the faces aligned near the ends of the slab. Align the ends of the slabs. This is part of maintaining the mirror image. By keeping the ends aligned, each component of the bookmatch will be directly across from its match in the other piece.

10 Use 2" rigid foam for clamp pads as you glue up the top. Rigid foam cushions the live edge from the clamps but provides enough flex to not mar the edge.

End grain alignment is also important if you're planning on leaving the existing ends on the slabs.

With the clamps snug, but not tight, tap the end grain with a mallet to bring the slabs into alignment. Allow any glue squeeze out to dry until it's rubbery and slice it off with a putty knife, **Photo 12**. The time it takes to get to this point will vary depending on your shop conditions, but it's usually around fifteen minutes after the glue-up. If you touch the squeeze out with your putty knife and it's runny, you haven't waited long enough. Using the putty knife too soon will smear wet glue all over the surface. If you wait too long the glue will get too hard to easily remove. The glue will easily slice away from the wood when it has dried to the right consistency. Allow the glue joint to cure and remove the clamps.

11 Bridge the glue seam with a clamp to hold the faces even. Align the ends of the slabs.

12 Remove glue squeeze out by slicing it off the surface with a putty knife after the glue gets rubbery.

Cut to Length and Mount Legs

If you're leaving the tabletop with its existing ends, you won't need to do a final length cut on it. Otherwise, mark the layout lines for the final length of the slab, **Photo 13**, and make the cuts with a jig saw or circular saw, **Photo 14**. A track saw can be used but isn't necessary, since the ends can be sanded after they're cut. The cut doesn't have to be perfectly straight. In fact, if the opposite end is being left with the original chainsaw cut (like this tabletop), it may look better to have an angled or curved cut. Experiment with different layouts to see what you prefer before making the cut.

Position the legs on the bottom face of the tabletop and mark out the mounting hole locations, **Photo 15**. The bolt holes in the legs are elongated slots, **Photo 16**, to allow the top to seasonally expand and contract. The fasteners should be placed in the middle of the slot to allow maximum movement.

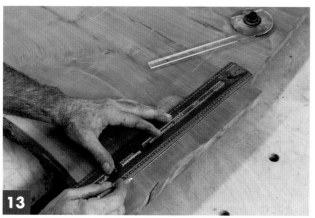

13

Lay out the final length of the tabletop. It doesn't have to be cut square.

14

Cut the slab to its finished length. A circular saw or jig saw works fine for this.

15

Locate the leg set on the bottom of the table. Mark the hole locations.

16

Slots in the legs allow for expansion and contraction of the top.

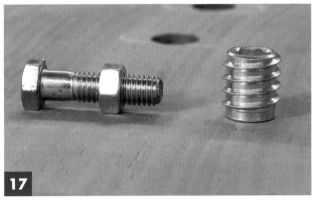

17

One method of mounting the legs is a threaded insert, right. The insert is screwed into the table and accepts a bolt.

Threaded inserts, **Photo 17**, are a great way to fasten legs to tables. The insert is threaded into the tabletop and the legs are secured using bolts. If the table needs to be moved the legs can easily be removed. This is especially handy on large slab tables. Wood screws or lag screws as an alternative form of fastening legs can also be removed. Doing so repeatedly, however, can weaken the grab the screw has on the tabletop.

Threaded inserts provide a stronger connection than screws. Follow the manufacturer's instructions on what size hole to drill for the insert. It's best to drill the holes using a portable drill guide, **Photo 18**, to ensure the hole is straight and drilled to the right depth. Drill the holes in the center of the elongated slots you marked out. Thread a nut onto the bolt, tighten it against the threaded insert, and apply a little paste wax on the insert threads, **Photo 19**. The

18

Use a portable drill guide to drill for the inserts. The drill guide helps keep the hole straight and includes a stop that controls the depth of the hole.

paste wax makes it easier to drive the insert in, and the nut allows you to use a ratchet, **Photo 20**, to thread the inserts into the holes. Drive the insert slightly below the surface of the wood, **Photo 21**, use a wrench to loosen the nut, and back out the bolt.

Add paste wax to the threads of the insert to make it easier to drive in.

Use a ratchet to drive the inserts in, being very careful to keep the insert going straight.

Drive the insert until it's slightly below the surface of the wood.

Sand and Finish

Sharp bark on the edge of a table, **Photo 22**, could make sitting close to the edge uncomfortable. A flutter sander will soften the edges a little but may not remove enough material. Instead of completely removing the bark with a draw knife, use a disc sander mounted in a drill to knock down the sharp edges, **Photo 23**. Start with 80-grit sandpaper. The disc sander allows you to free form shape the edge, maintaining the organic look of the original bark edge.

Sharp edges can make it uncomfortable to sit at a table and should be softened slightly with some sanding.

After the edges have been shaped, sand them, and the rest of the table, using a random orbit sander. Apply your choice of finish. Remember to finish the top and bottom faces of the table. After the finish is dry, secure the legs to the bottom of the table, **Photo 24**. Grab a buddy to help you flip over the table and enjoy a feast.

23

Sand off the sharp live edges with a disc sander, and then sand the entire slab using a random orbit sander.

24

Place the tabletop upside down on a bench and fasten the legs. Be sure to use pads on the bench to protect the top face.

Resources

Moisture Meter
Lignomat Ligno-Scanner D
lignomatusa.com

Slab flattening
Woodpeckers Slab Flattening Mill
woodpeck.com

Mop sander
2" x 6" Sand Mop
woodworkingshop.com

Epoxy pigment
mixol.com

Mica powder
Amazon.com

Rare Earth Magnets
Neodymium Bar Magnets
5 mm x 10 mm x 60 mm
Amazon.com

Bowtie inlay kit
Cut the pocket and the inlay
Rockler.com
Mlcswoodworking.com
Woodcraft.com
Cut the pocket, get the inlay
from the manufacturer. Deer
track inlay, brass inlay
Slabstitcher.com

Trammel points
Rockler.com

Tabletop fasteners
Rockler.com

30" C Thru Flex Curve
Woodcraft.com

Epoxy syringe
Amazon.com

MatchFit Clamps
Microjig.com

Floating shelf hardware
Woodworking stores, online
Used here, Rose's Rustics Heavy
Duty Floating Shelf Brackets
Amazon.com

Magnetic featherboard
Magswitch Universal
Featherboard Pro
Magswitch.com

Extra-long drill bits
Amazon.com

Dining table legs
Bearhollowsupply.com

Height of furniture

As you're developing projects you'll find it useful to know the typical heights of various pieces so you can determine leg length

Benches	18" – 20"
Coffee tables	Same height or 2" lower than adjacent couch seat, typically 10" – 18"
Desk	28" – 30"
Dining tables	28" – 30"
End tables	The height of the arm of the nearest chair or sofa, typically 24" – 32"

About the Author

George Vondriska has been teaching woodworking since 1986. In addition to running his own woodworking school, George has taught woodworking courses for woodworking shows, woodworking schools, retail stores, the U.S. Peace Corps, the Pentagon, Northwest Airlines, and Andersen Windows. George also teaches in-person classes at his shop, Vondriska Woodworks.

You may also know George from his work as the tools and new products editor for *American Woodworker* Magazine, his articles in *Fine Woodworking*, *WOOD*, and *Woodworkers Journal* magazines, or from his current position as managing editor of *WoodWorkers Guild of America*, where he teaches all kinds of techniques and projects on video.

You can learn more about George at *vondriskawoodworks.com* or on Instagram and Facebook @vondriskaworks

Index

Note: Page numbers in *italics* indicate projects.